Up Your Teaching Game

Creating Story-Based Games to Engage K-12 Students

Janna Jackson Kellinger

Routledge
Taylor & Francis Group
NEW YORK AND LONDON

Designed cover image: © Getty Images

First published 2025
by Routledge
605 Third Avenue, New York, NY 10158

and by Routledge
4 Park Square, Milton Park, Abingdon, Oxon, OX14 4RN

Routledge is an imprint of the Taylor & Francis Group, an informa business

© 2025 Janna Jackson Kellinger

The right of Janna Jackson Kellinger to be identified as author of this work has been asserted in accordance with sections 77 and 78 of the Copyright, Designs and Patents Act 1988.

All rights reserved. No part of this book may be reprinted or reproduced or utilised in any form or by any electronic, mechanical, or other means, now known or hereafter invented, including photocopying and recording, or in any information storage or retrieval system, without permission in writing from the publishers.

Trademark notice: Product or corporate names may be trademarks or registered trademarks, and are used only for identification and explanation without intent to infringe.

Library of Congress Cataloging-in-Publication Data
Names: Kellinger, Janna Jackson, author.
Title: Up your teaching game : creating story-based games to engage K-12 students / Janna Jackson Kellinger.
Description: New York, NY : Routledge, 2025. | Includes bibliographical references.
Identifiers: LCCN 2024040576 (print) | LCCN 2024040577 (ebook) | ISBN 9781032575209 (hardback) |
ISBN 9781032576183 (paperback) | ISBN 9781003584308 (ebook)
Subjects: LCSH: Teaching--Aids and devices. | Storytelling in education. | Video games in education. | Curriculum planning.
Classification: LCC LB1044.88 .K45 2025 (print) |
LCC LB1044.88 (ebook) | DDC 371.33--dc23/eng/20241104
LC record available at https://lccn.loc.gov/2024040576
LC ebook record available at https://lccn.loc.gov/2024040577

ISBN: 978-1-032-57520-9 (hbk)
ISBN: 978-1-032-57618-3 (pbk)
ISBN: 978-1-003-58430-8 (ebk)

DOI: 10.4324/9781003584308

Typeset in Palatino
by SPi Technologies India Pvt Ltd (Straive)

Up Your Teaching Game

Creating Story-Based Games to Engage K-12 Students

Up Your Teaching Game offers K–12 teachers an intuitive and refreshingly fun pathway for creating immersive, story-based games that encourage students to experience the curriculum through play. Regardless of their technical abilities, design acumen, grade level, or domain, today's teachers have fresh opportunities to create and implement their own content-based games based on the same techniques that video game designers use to create commercial video games. In five actionable steps, this book prepares educators to design curricular games that teach instead of test, that are derived from content rather than divergent from it, and that motivate students to take ownership over their learning. Programs that most teachers are familiar with, such as PowerPoint and Google Slides, and technologies that may be new to them, such as Twine and Scratch, are addressed alongside the use of their own classrooms and schools as game spaces. Novice and veteran teachers alike, as well as curriculum designers and school technologists, will find a wealth of strategies and lessons learned, tips for avoiding pitfalls and time constraints, examples of quests and storyline advancement, and much more.

Janna Jackson Kellinger is Professor in the College of Education and Human Development at the University of Massachusetts Boston, USA.

Also Available from Routledge Eye On Education
(www.routledge.com/k-12)

Teaching in the Game-Based Classroom: Practical Strategies for Grades 6-12
Edited By David Seelow

Making Technology Work in Schools: How PK-12 Educators Can Foster Digital-Age Learning
Timothy D. Green, Loretta C. Donovan, Jody Peerless Green

Artificial Intelligence in Schools: A Guide for Teachers, Administrators, and Technology Leaders
Varun Arora

The Teacher's Guide to Scratch – Beginner: Professional Development for Coding Education
Kai Hutchence

The Teacher's Guide to Scratch – Intermediate: Professional Development for Coding Education
Kai Hutchence

The Teacher's Guide to Scratch – Advanced: Professional Development for Coding Education
Kai Hutchence

Up Your Teaching Game: Creating Story-Based Games to Engage K-12 Students
Janna Jackson Kellinger

For my students—you have made this work both possible and pleasurable

Contents

Acknowledgments viii

1 Beginning Your Journey 1

2 Introducing the Story-Based Game Design Process 20

3 Creating the Characters (Somebody) 52

4 Developing Goals (Wanted) 78

5 Designing the Game Obstacles (But) 99

6 Implementing the Core Game Mechanic (So) 117

7 Orchestrating the End Game (Then) 146

8 Achievement Unlocked! 156

Glossary 168

Acknowledgments

As with any book, the author is just a conduit for a lifetime of learning. For me, that learning has occurred at the hands of my students, my colleagues, others who have written in this field, presenters at conferences, and others. That learning, however, has also derived from playing, observing, and discussing games with my own children. Their insight and wisdom constantly astonish me. However, it is my sister whom I have to thank the most for playtesting my coding course and "playtesting" this book. She has been my tireless editor, go-to person, and advocate. Her support and suggestions mean so much to me. Thank you, Julia Nakhleh, for your time, your patience, and your insight. This book would not have been possible without you.

1

Beginning Your Journey

Groggily you come to. You try to move but you realize you are handcuffed and gagged. Slowly you remember being ambushed in your lab and being knocked out by a large person with a chair. "They must be trying to get my new invention," you think. You suspected that once word got out, villains would want to get their hands on this powerful new tool, you just didn't think it would happen this quickly. You know **you must prevent them at all costs***. After all, whoever controls this new technological invention can rule the world.*

(Kellinger, *Coding for Non-Coders Class*, 2022)

Imagine your students being totally captivated by your curriculum, excited for the next lesson and even being motivated to do their own research to enhance their learning. Think about how engaged some students are with videogames, spending hours and hours on them. Imagine if you could capture some of that magic for your classwork. This book introduces you to a way to do so by exploring how to convert your curriculum into a story-based game. To begin, let me tell you a little bit about my own journey as an educator.

I have been a teacher for over 30 years, teaching all four high school grade levels, as well as undergraduate and graduate students at four different schools and in three different states. While I have had mostly positive reviews, it hasn't been until recently that students have described being "addicted" to my courses.

In course evaluations, survey responses, and emails to me, students describe being "hooked" on my classes, saying they find it hard to stop doing the work once they start or tell me about their "aha" moments or that they "LOVE" my class, with many students using both "fun" and "challenging" to describe my courses. I wish I could say this is because I am a charismatic teacher, but that's not why students "rave" about my courses. Students enjoy my classes because, as several have said, they want to find out what happens in the story. You are probably thinking I mistyped and meant to say "in the class" instead of "in the story." However, the two are the same. I teach all my classes by creating game-stories that students can play, and in the reading and playing of the story, they learn the course content and skills. The goal of this book is to teach you how to do the same.

You can see by the bolding in the excerpt from my most recent game-based course that the game-story creates the suspense that drives students to want to keep going, in this case because they want to find out if the thieves are prevented from getting this dangerous new invention, what the new invention is, and why it is so dangerous! How I got to this point in my teaching was not easy. Along the way, I made some pretty ugly mistakes. My hope is that you will learn from my successes as well as my failures as you read through my journey from being a student teacher who had an "epic fail" when trying to review using a *Jeopardy* game to one who now designs game-based courses. Let's start from the beginning.

> **ACTION ITEM**: Where would you put yourself on a scale of "never played any games with my students" to "played competitive games as part of a lesson" to "played a game that took place over several lessons" to "designed a game-based course"? Where would you like to be? What do you hope to get out of this book?

How Did My Game-Based Teaching Evolve?

If you are like me, there are memories from your student teaching that stand out like they happened yesterday, even after decades of being in a classroom. One of my moments was when I tried having a review day for a test by having students play *Jeopardy*. Nowadays, teachers have all sorts of apps they can use to do this, but back then, all I had was chalk and a chalkboard. I drew the *Jeopardy* matrix on the board, complete with categories and the amounts and was all ready for the students, or at least I thought I was. When students started slapping in and shouting out answers, I couldn't tell who answered first and chaos ensued as arguments erupted. In addition, with my back turned to the students half the time as I tried to keep track of everything on the chalkboard, little did I realize that students were lobbing wadded-up pieces of paper out the window. When the vice principal came charging into the classroom demanding to know why it was "snowing" in April in Durham, North Carolina, I almost quit teaching right then and there. Fortunately, I stuck with teaching and, like so many other failures in my teaching career, this moment radically shifted the way I approached teaching.

After that debacle, I vowed never to use a *Jeopardy* game in my classroom again. However, I relented after a few years, but this time, I discovered the importance that rules play in games. In this new version, each group had a designated spokesperson who had 60 seconds to give an answer. Instead of having groups slap in all at once, each group had their turn. If a group didn't get an answer correct, the question went to the next group, giving all students an incentive to pay attention. This version of *Jeopardy* worked a lot more smoothly, and subsequently, I incorporated a lot of other "one-shot" games like this into my teaching. I discovered that chalkboards are magnetic and put magnets on the back of sentence strips so students could compete to rearrange items on the board,[1] such as putting an MLA citation in the correct order. We also played "last one standing" games, such as one where students had to give an example of a part of speech that began with the last letter of the previous example and were out if they couldn't. And we played a game where students got a pop quiz unless the class could successfully answer five reading comprehension questions. While students had fun, I felt like something was missing.

I slowly came to realize that all these games weren't about learning. They were really about recall. In other words, they were just tests dressed up as games. In addition, most of them relied on some students being losers. I wanted something more. I wanted all my students to be winners. At the same time, I was playing *Myst* adventure games, which are deeply immersive story-based videogames with lots of in-game puzzles to solve. My initial thought was that videogame designers should incorporate educational content into videogames. Then my epiphany came when I realized that, since students were going home and spending endless hours learning from videogames—hours they certainly were not spending on my homework, it wasn't videogame designers who needed to change, but rather educators. Laura Devaney (2014) captures this phenomenon best when she describes kids quitting homework when it's too hard while quitting videogames when they are too easy. I longed to create courses where my students learned from having "hard fun" (McGonigal, 2011), just like how I learned from playing videogames—learning how new worlds operate, learning how to solve puzzles, and learning new strategies. The idea that videogames were the key to teaching "total immersion" courses percolated in the back of my mind for quite a while but did not come to fruition until I became a college professor.

Years later, when I was teaching an educational technology course at a university, I had another big failure that also ended up radically altering my teaching. Instead of giving students the freedom to explore, I told them step-by-step what to do. Students were bored out of their minds. I was bored out of my mind. There was no creativity. This was driven home by a student comment on RateMyProfessor.com that said, "I found the class to be very long and boring and left with very little knowledge other than the fact that if you use AIM Chat on a different computer, it changes your buddy icon." I vowed never to teach an ed tech class again, and once again, I relented. However, the next time I taught an ed tech class, I taught it as a semester-long game. After that awful class, I had been thinking about how to make my classes more gamelike, but my real breakthrough came when I learned about Barnard College's *Reacting to the Past* classes, which are courses structured around semester-long, role-playing games. Prior to that, I hadn't even conceived of a whole course being a game.

With a new passion, I set out to create a game-based course. This time, instead of *pushing* content onto students, I created challenges so students would want to *pull* content to solve them.[2] While my first game-based course came with much more positive reviews, with students stating they learned a lot while having fun, and my course evaluation scores rose tremendously,[3] I violated the KISS principle—Keep It Simple, Stupid. My complicated storyline was fine for teaching the class in person, as I could have students work in groups and coach them in the moment, but when I converted it to an online class, I realized pretty quickly that I had overly complicated the game-story, which involved a principal hiring a private detective to go undercover as a new teacher to discover who defaced her Facebook page by communicating with a student whom the principal planted as a mole, but the private detective did not know which student was the mole for the student's protection, so the private detective had to use newly learned content area literacy skills to secretly pass codes and get intelligence from the student mole. It's exhausting just writing out the backstory!

As I created more and more game-based courses, I learned more about how to design them to maximize what Csikszentmihalyi (1990) calls *flow*, a state of total immersion, by keeping students in the challenge zone. As educators, we know this as Vygotsky's (1978) "Zone of Proximal Development" (ZPD)—designing learning activities that aren't too easy and aren't too hard. As my game-based courses evolved, so did my approach to designing them. I wrote a book in 2017 titled *A Guide to Designing Curricular Games: How to "Game" the System* that extolled the virtues of using systems-based thinking in designing game-based courses, and I taught an Introduction to Game-Based Teaching course based on this process. However, I found that the systems design process did not work as effectively as I had hoped for my students who were aspiring K–12 teachers. Just like with my first game-based course, I overly complicated the process. Going back to the drawing board, I realized that the crux of designing game-based courses was in creating the game-story itself.

What Is a Game?

Before we dive into that new process, it is helpful to step back for a moment to come to a shared understanding of what a game is. Sid Meier, creator of *Civilization*, describes games as "a series of interesting choices" (quoted by Prensky, 2011, p. 272). You could describe life as "a series of interesting choices," but I would argue that life is not a game. The difference between life and games lies in the real-world results of those decisions: "[I]t's better to make a mistake in a chemistry game than a chemistry lab" (a student quoted in Kellinger, 2017, p. 17). Games are fun because they lack IRL (in real life) consequences so you can try different actions to see how the game world responds.[4] In fact, some game-players make mistakes on purpose just to see what happens. I was observing one of my own children playing a videogame where clicking on the correct island advances you to the next level, but, because each wrong island had an interesting response such as actually being the top of a sea monster or being an island of pirates, he would figure out the right answer first so he could save the correct island for last, allowing him to explore all the wrong islands before moving on. He was doing the mental work of figuring out the correct answer but doing so in order to make mistakes on purpose. Because there are no IRL consequences and because losing to a computer is not as shameful as losing to a human, players can test out the boundaries of the game world and experiment to their heart's content, knowing they can always retry. In fact, consistently, the most praised aspect of my game-based classes on course evaluations is the ability to revise and resubmit, something that is necessary for a game-based class that is based on mastery progression but can also exist in non-game-based classes as well. I contend that the cycle of trying something out, getting feedback, and making changes accordingly drives the learning process—and drives gameplay in videogames.

Science teachers will recognize what I just described as the bare bones of the scientific method—developing a hypothesis, testing it, making changes to your hypothesis based on the results, and testing again. It is also the cycle that English teachers use when teaching writing—students submit rough drafts, English teachers give feedback, students make changes, and so forth. Same with math classes that require students to show their work. This process of hypothesizing, testing, revising, and trying again can be expanded to apply to any number of subjects, including game design. So what is it about games that make this process fun and not laborious? I contend that the difference between traditional schooling and gameplaying hinges on three aspects of games that often are not present in traditional classrooms:

1) A game-story
2) Mastery-based leveling up
3) Retrying without real-world consequences

Let's briefly explore each of these.

First of all, the game-story. I know what you are thinking: *Tetris*, the videogame where players have to fit falling shapes into a wall, does not have a game-story.[5] And you are correct. Not all games have game-stories. You could make up a story to explain a game like *Tetris*, but that would be a false imposition. These non-story games tend to be casual games, games you play while you are waiting for a bus or in a doctor's waiting room because you can stop playing at the drop of a hat. They rate high on aspects two (mastery-based leveling up) and three (retrying) but lack number one, a game-story. They are really good at getting players to learn and improve a discrete skill. For our purposes, we will call these types of games "mini-games." There's nothing wrong with these casual mini-games. In fact, if that's your goal—improving a discrete skill—then, by all means, have your students play mini-games. This book, however, will show you how you can embed these mini-games into your game-story so that your students can *experience* your curriculum instead of just being exposed to it.

While stories are immersive, in his book *Theory of Fun*, Koster (2014) argues that stories can only take you so far because they lack the second aspect of games: mastery-based leveling up, in other words, moving on to harder challenges contingent upon successfully completing easier challenges. According to Koster (2014), because games offer us an opportunity to practice and learn from our mistakes,

> A book will never be able to accelerate the grokking process [i.e., mastering a skill to the point of intuition] to the degree that games do because you cannot practice a pattern and run permutations on it with a book, and have the book respond with feedback.
>
> (p. 38)

It is this aspect of games that provides "a model [of] how to optimize the learning curve so that the user's skills are gradually tested and balanced with increasing challenges" (Mayra, 2008, p. 54). Constantly keeping players in the challenge zone is what makes games so addictive, while the game-story is what "renders the skills learned by players meaningful" (Malone, 1981, quoted in Games & Squire, 2011, p. 21). As McGonigal (2011) observes, in games, "[e]veryone can level up as long as they keep working hard" (p. 130), which points out a fundamental difference between games and traditional schooling: failure in games signals "not yet," whereas in traditional schooling, it's "now or never."

The third aspect, retrying without real-world consequences, is what adds the fun to games because players can safely take risks. As the protagonist in the fictional *Mortality Doctrine* series states,

> Even the most brutal games in the VirtNet were played with the knowledge that dying was just a setback. Nothing more than a delay. And that helped people go out there and play without reserve, taking chances and doing things they'd *never* do in real life. That was what made it fun—you could always go back and try again.
> (Dashner, 2013, p. 167)

It is this ability to take risks that makes gaming fun. And it is the ability to make mistakes and have the chance to try again that allows players to take these risks that make games "deliberate practice machines" (Koster, 2014, p. 100). When you compare that to traditional schooling, where a mistake often means a bad grade with no chance of trying again, you can see why students would prefer gaming over schooling.

So, for our purposes, games are playable stories where players can try the challenges as many times as needed in order to succeed, and success leads to mastery-based leveling up. Revisiting these three aspects of games, we see that stories add the immersion, mastery-based leveling up adds the addiction, and retrying adds the fun. These three words—immersion, addiction, and fun—are rarely included in students' descriptions of their schooling experiences. However, all three of these words have been used in student course evaluations to describe students' experiences taking my classes. This book lays out how you, too, can design your courses to be immersive, addictive, and fun.

What Are the Differences between Gamification, Game-Based Learning, and Game-Based Teaching?

Now that we've established what distinguishes games from traditional teaching, let's explore how they can be used in the classroom to turn traditional teaching on its head. You have probably heard the terms "gamification," "game-based learning," and "game-based teaching." You may have even heard them used interchangeably. However, there are differences among gamifying teaching, game-based learning, and game-based teaching. Gamifying teaching, or "gamification," uses game terms to rename traditional practices. Grades become "experience points," stickers become "badges," student groups become "guilds." Just like this book is not about dressing up tests as games, this book is also not about gamification.

Game-based learning, on the other hand, uses premade games as instructional tools. There has been a lot written about how teachers can use commercial games to teach. This ranges from building digital dioramas in *Minecraft* to using recall-based games like *Kahoot* to gamelike software dubbed "edutainment" that uses gaming to various degrees to test students' knowledge. *Duolingo*, a popular language learning app, straddles gamification and game-based learning by using in-game rewards as motivation, but the learning itself tends to be rote. Out of curiosity, one of my own children chose English in *Duolingo*, even though he already knows English, to see what that would be like. A lot of the sentences were about long-distance relationships (which shows you who their demographic is). Think about how much more engaging this would be as a story where the player is trying to woo a character in the game by speaking in their language and, if they do well, eventually win them over. While some of these education games are much more like my "one-shot" recall games from when I taught high school, some of these games are powerful learning tools, such as *Lure of the Labyrinth*, which teaches pre-algebra skills through various challenges within the context of a game-story. Others are "broccoli and chocolate games" (Laurel, 2001) — games where students have to answer drill and skill problems (the "broccoli") in order to receive the reward of playing a game (the "chocolate"). As Klopfer et al. (2009) state, "If your spaceship requires you to answer a math problem before you can use your blasters, chances are you'll hate the game and the math" (p. 25). The difference between these types of "edutainment" games and game-based learning is that powerful learning games "find the game in the content" (Klopfer, et al., 2009, p. 31). If you find a premade game that suits your teaching goals, immerses students, has mastery-based leveling up, and is fun, by all means, use it!

Chances are, however, that you won't be able to find premade games for every topic you teach. This book lays out a process that teachers can use to design their own story-based learning games. Like premade games, we want our learning games to be immersive, challenging, and fun. I have found the best way to do this is to embed the learning in a game-story. While some non-story-based games can be fun, they tend to be competition-style recall games. For example, I just read an article about having a "Family-Feud style" cybersecurity game (Zugar, 2024) where players compete to try to guess the top ten answers in a survey about cybersecurity, and I thought, "What a lost opportunity!" Think about how much fun it would be to play a story-based game where players have to protect their data or, better yet, hack into a system by exploiting its flaws.

In order to ensure that the curricular content is seen as a tool and not an obstacle, these game-stories must be derived from the curricular content. In a book chapter I wrote for *The Handbook of College Reading and Study Strategies* (2018), I describe a three-prong test for this. One of those prongs I call "content-swapping." If the player has to solve fraction equations correctly in order for the monster to open a gate, that game is not derived from the content because you can swap in any other content—for example, the monster could ask questions about American history. However, if the player has to understand how fractions add up to a whole to solve the locking mechanism on a gate to open it or, better yet, how to use ratios to make the potion that causes the monster to fall asleep at the gate, then the learning itself is embedded into the game-story as an instrument, not an impediment. The goal of this book is to explore a process for designing your own content-driven learning games, in other words, game-based teaching.

Does Game-based Teaching Work?

Because of the conflation of gamification, game-based learning, and game-based teaching and the diversity within each of those categories, it is difficult to come to definitive conclusions based on research studies. However, meta-analyses (studies of studies) do suggest that game-based teaching does increase student learning more so than traditional instruction (Clark et al., 2016; Connolly et al., 2012; Sitzmann, 2011; Vogel et al., 2006; Wouters et al., 2013). These results indicate that using games to learn increases knowledge retention, comprehension, and skills (Boller and Kapp, 2017, p. 23). We can infer, then, that it is the active, or rather interactive, nature of games that allows them to beat out more passive forms of learning, such as listening to a lecture. In other words, games produce learning, whereas reading and listening involve consuming content.

At the other end of the spectrum from meta-analyses are anecdotes about how games teach, such as this one:

> When asked what helped him make the transition between basketball and football, Antonio Gates, an All-Pro NFL tight end, told *Sports Illustrated* (Silver, 2004): "You know what helped? Playing *Madden*. I was always the Chargers. After I go there, I'd play the game and notice things about the defenses. I started recognizing formations in the [video] game, then I'd get to practice and see them there [in actual practice]."
>
> (Squire, 2011, p. 11)

In between meta-analyses and anecdotes are research case studies. In one, Squire (2011) found that students taught via traditional methods regurgitated facts while those who played a game exhibited deeper understanding. When a student in the control group was asked why he drew the electric field around a positive charge the way he did, he replied, "I don't know. The teacher said so and showed us a picture and that was what it looked like," whereas a student in the experimental group who played a learning game about the same topic said:

> The electric field goes from the positive charge to the negative charge like this [drawing a curved line from a positive charge to a negative charge]. This is what it looked like in the game, and it was hard to move away or toward it because the two charges are close together, so they sort of cancel each other out.
>
> (Squire, 2011, p. 98)

By focusing on experiencing the curriculum instead of being subjected to it, games help students make connections that lead to deeper learning.

There is some indication that gameplaying itself changes mindsets: "Beck and Wade (2004) surveyed thousands of young workers and showed that gamers were more likely to prefer self-directed learning, experimentation and failure, and searching out experts on a topic" (Squire, 2011, p. 163). The conclusions of a compilation of studies on learning (National Academies of Science, Engineering, and Medicine, 2018) support this constructivist approach to learning. This report goes on to describe optimal learning environments by stating that learners should have opportunities to "make logical connections between pieces of information" and "apply [mental representations] to new contexts" in "nonthreatening" environments that "promote a sense of agency and purpose" (pp. 5–6). This certainly sounds like what games do! In fact, the report itself cites leveling up in videogames as a way to create intrinsic motivation to learn (p. 116) and singles out the interactivity of games as a way to promote learning (p. 165). It adds that adaptivity, choice, and feedback all support learning (p. 165). While the report cautions that gameplaying shows only a "moderate" improvement in learning as compared to traditional methods, it bases this largely on Mayer's 2014 meta-analysis, which includes learning games often deemed "edutainment."

The answer to "Does game-based teaching work?" lies in matching the game to the educational goal. If the goal is for students to regurgitate content on a test, then a recall game is best. If it is to improve a specific skill, then employ a mastery-based, mini-game focused on that skill. If it is for students to learn how to problem-solve, strategy games may be the key. However, as Roussos and Dovidio (2016) point out, sometimes intended goals are not actualized goals, as they found that the game *Spent*, which was supposed to teach empathy toward people who have lower incomes, ended up cementing people's assumption that poor people are poor because they don't make good decisions since there is a way to make it to the end of the month and pay all the bills in the game. So, the real answer to "Does game-based teaching work?" is to playtest your curricular game to see if it achieves your learning objectives. In other words, what we already do with our teaching—try something out, get feedback from our students, and make adjustments. Huh. That sounds a lot like how games are played!

Conclusion

What is more powerful to me than the results of any research study is evidence from my own students. Based on years of teaching game-based courses, students have consistently reported that not only have they enjoyed these courses, they have learned a lot, including a student who began my Coding for Non-coders course with no knowledge of coding. She said that, from taking this course, she learned that anything is possible, even when you think you can't do it. In addition, students who have taken my Introduction to Game-Based Teaching course have successfully used games in their own teaching, so much so that a reporter tracked down several of them who are now K–12 teachers for an article on game-based teaching. In the article, one of my former students is quoted as saying, "I see a lot more class engagement when we are doing games," and another explains he found that of those students whose engagement tends to lag in class, "[Y]ou see them start to take a larger role in the class and they seem more driven and interested in the material" (Camero, 2022). Based on my success and the successes of others, designing curricular games is worth a try. I have always viewed teaching and learning as experimental. I encourage you to experiment with your teaching to see what works in your content and context and for your students.

Chapter 1 Worksheet: Game Reflections

Directions: Play five new games. These could be videogames, card games, board games, or sports games. Choose games that are very different from each other. As you play, think about what content and skills you are learning. It might help to reflect after gameplay on what you know and can do now that you couldn't before you played. Then, reflect on how you learned that content and skills and if the learning was fun. If so, what made it fun? Fill out the following worksheet with your thoughts. Return to this throughout the game design process for inspiration.

Name of game played	What you learned	How you learned	What made it fun

Notes

1. This was my primitive version of a SmartBoard.
2. This concept of pushing and pulling comes from Rabone (2013, p. 2).
3. For more details about this first game-based course, see Jackson (2009). (Jackson is my maiden name).
4. Huizinga (1955). calls this the "magic circle" of games.
5. While you could claim **Tetris** tells a bare-bones story about building, you would be hard-pressed to really identify story elements like a protagonist, setting, climax, and denouement. However, Janet Murray (1997) argues that **Tetris** is the "perfect enactment of the overtasked lives of Americans in the 1990s—of the constant bombardment of tasks that demand our attention and that we must somehow fit into our overcrowded schedules and clear off our desks in order to make room for the next onslaught.... Tetris allows us to symbolically experience agency over our lives" (p. 144).

References

Beck, J. C., & Wade, M. (2004). *Got game: How the gamer generation is reshaping business forever.* Cambridge, MA: Harvard Business Press.

Boller, S. & Kapp, K. (2017). *Play to learn: Everything you need to know about designing effective learning games.* Alexandria, VA: ATD Press.

Camero, H. (2022). Game based learning and videogames as teaching tools catching on with MA schools. *Wicked Local.*

Clark D., Tanner-Smith E., & Killingsworth S. (2016). Digital games, design, and learning: A systematic review and meta-analysis. *Review of Educational Research, 86*(1), 79–122.

Connolly, T., Boyle, E., MacArthur, E., Hainey, T., & Boyle, J. (2012). A systematic literature review of empirical evidence on computer games and serious games. *Computers & Education, 59*(2), 661–686.

Csikszentmihalyi, M. (1990). *Flow: The psychology of optimal experience.* New York: Harper & Row.

Dashner, J. (2013). *The eye of minds.* New York: Random House.

Devaney, L. (2014, July 7). 5 gaming dynamics that truly engage students. *eSchoolNews*, at http://www.eschoolnews.com/2014/07/07/gaming-engaging-students-365/ [Retrieved November 6, 2015]

Games, A & Squire, K. (2011). Searching for the fun in learning. In S. Tobias and J.D. Fletcher (Eds.) *Computer games and instruction* (pp. 17–46). Charlotte, NC: Information Age Publishers.

Huizinga, J. (1955). Nature and significance of play as a cultural phenomenon from Homo Ludens: A study of the play element in culture. In K. Salen and E. Zimmerman (Eds.). *The game designer reader: A rules of play anthology* (pp. 96–120) Cambridge, MA: MIT Press.

Jackson, J. (2009). Game-based teaching: What educators can learn from videogames. *Teaching Education, 20*(3), 291–304.

Kellinger, J. (2022). *Coding for non-coders.* Course taught in the College of Education and Human Development at UMass Boston.

Kellinger, J. (2018). Gaming and college reading. In R. Flippo and T. Bean (Eds.). *Handbook of college reading and study strategy research* (3rd ed., pp. 168–177). New York: Taylor and Francis.

Kellinger, J. (2017). *A guide to designing curricular games: How to "game" the system*. Cham, Switzerland: Springer.

Klopfer, E., Osterweil, S., & Salen, K. (2009). *Moving learning games forward: Obstacles, opportunities, and openness*. Cambridge, MA: The Education Arcade at MIT.

Koster, R. (2014). *A Theory of fun for game design*. Sebastopol, CA: O'Reilly Media.

Laurel, B. (2001). *Utopian entrepreneur*. Cambridge: MIT Press.

Malone, T. W. (1981). Toward a theory of intrinsically motivating instruction. *Cognitive Science, 4*, 333–369.

Mayer, R. (2014). *Computer games for learning: An evidence-based approach*. Cambridge, MA: MIT Press.

Mayra, F. (2008). *An introduction to game studies*. Thousand Oaks, CA: Sage.

McGonigal, J. (2011). *Reality is broken: Why games make us better and how they can change the world*. London: Penguin Books.

Murray, J. (1997). *Hamlet on the holodeck: The future of narrative in cyberspace*. Cambridge, MA: MIT Press.

National Academies of Sciences, Engineering, and Medicine. (2018). *How People Learn II: Learners, Contexts, and Cultures*. Washington, DC: The National Academies Press.

Prensky, M. (2011). Comments on research comparing games to other instructional methods. In S. Tobias and J. D. Fletcher (Eds.), *Computer games and instruction*, (pp. 251–280). Charlotte, NC: Information Age Publishers.

Rabone, D. (2013). How "game mechanics" can revitalize education. *eSchoolNews*, at https://www.eschoolnews.com/top-news/2013/02/12/how-game-mechanics-can-revitalize-education/

Roussos, G., & Dovidio, J. F. (2016). Playing below the poverty line: Investigating an online game as a way to reduce prejudice toward the poor. *Cyberpsychology: Journal of Psychosocial Research on Cyberspace, 10*(2), Article 3.

Silver, M. (2004 December 13). Stepping out. *Sports Illustrated*.

Sitzmann, T. (2011). A meta-analytic examination of the instructional effectiveness of computer-based simulation games. *Personnel Psychology, 64*, 489–528.

Squire, K. (2011). *Videogames and learning: Teaching and participatory culture in the digital age*. NY: Teachers College Press.

Vogel, J. J., Vogel, D. S., Cannon-Bowers, J., Bowers, C. A., Muse, K., & Wright, M. (2006). Computer gaming and interactive simulations for learning: A meta-analysis. *Journal of Educational Computing Research, 34*, 229–243.

Vygotsky, L. (1978). *Mind in society*. Cambridge, MA: Harvard University Press.

Wouters, P., van Nimwegen, C., van Oostendorp, H., & van der Spek, E. D. (2013). A meta-analysis of the cognitive and motivational effects of serious games. *Journal of Educational Psychology, 105*, 249–265.

Zugar, S. (2024, July 15). Gamifying cybersecurity training. *Tech & Learning*, at https://www.techlearning.com/news/gamifying-cybersecurity-training [Retrieved July 17, 2024].

2

Introducing the Story-Based Game Design Process

*Thank you for coming in today. I'm Agent Smith from the FBI. You might remember me from your hospital room. We appreciate you sharing your invention with us, however, I come with disturbing news. I need to speak with you confidentially. Since you trusted me, I feel I can trust you. What I'm about to say cannot leave this room. There is a growing concern in the agency that the current president is using your invention to further her own ends. Obviously, as president of the United States, she had to be told of this powerful tool. There is some evidence, though, that she is using the ability to mentally control technology to line her own pockets and there is fear she will use it to rig the next election to keep herself in power. As you can see, if this proves to be true, this endangers our democracy. I come to you to seek your help in finding out if this is the case and, if so, disabling her capability so she won't become a dictator. In other words, we want you to destroy your own invention. Now that it's in the government's hands, this will mean **using your coding skills** to infiltrate the most impenetrable part of the U.S. government—the Pentagon.*

(Kellinger, *Coding for Beginners Trailer*, 2022)

The story snippet appears in the form of an animated video at the end of my coding class where the game-story revolves around saving the player's invention—technological telepathy—from thieves. It is meant to be a teaser to entice students to take the follow-up class. While I have not designed that follow-up class as of the writing of this book, when asked after viewing the trailer, 90% of my students said they would take the sequel class. More than one student even said they wanted to take it, but unfortunately, they are graduating. Notice that, at this point, there is no game, just the beginnings of a story, but a story that suggests a game—that of hacking into the Pentagon. What made this preview so compelling that students wanted to pursue it, the story or the game? This leads to the age-old question in videogame design—which is more important, the game or the story. I argue, however, that you cannot separate the two.

Over the course of the evolution of my game-based courses, I wavered from the story serving as a framework on which to hang the game activities, like in my overly complicated course with the private detective posing as a new teacher, to being very story focused with the content of the course embedded in the narrative, such as the conversations among characters in my curriculum design course where students play as a new teacher and each of the veteran teachers represents a different curricular ideology, to courses that were really a series of mini-games with a loose storyline that faded into the background, such as my Human Development course where each unit has a game-like simulation based on that week's developmental approach. This vacillation represents a long-standing controversy in videogame design—ludology (gameplay) versus narratology (game-story). The approach that I found most successful is to merge both, where the gameplay and the storyline are tightly interwoven such as in the course that I currently teach where students have to code their way out of the situation they are in. The thrust of this approach is to develop a game-story that derives from the content of the course and drives the gameplay, in other words, "playable stories."

> **ACTION ITEM**: Take one of the games you played in the first chapter. How would you make it into a story? Then, think of a story you like. How would you make it a game? Which is better? Why? Is there a way you could create something that integrates the best of both versions?

Why Are Stories So Pedagogically Powerful?

Because humans tend to organize their understandings of the world based on stories, stories are a powerful teaching medium. Ask anyone to tell you how they became their profession. Instead of reciting their resumé, most people will tell you a story with a beginning, middle, and end. Most ancient cultures have a mythology or stories invented in order to explain scientific phenomena. In my own life, the power of stories was demonstrated when my father insisted he had already seen the second Harry Potter movie because he remembered the story when, in fact, he had not seen the movie but rather heard me read it to him when he was in the hospital after having had a stroke. It turned out he had no recollection of me reading the book to him, but he remembered the plot of the story. Stories stick with us. Stories resonate with us. Stories help us make sense of our own experiences and the experiences of others.

Brain studies show that when people read stories, they experience it vicariously: "[T]he brain, it seems, does not make much of a distinction between reading about an experience and encountering it in real life; in each case, the same neurological regions are stimulated" (Paul, 2012, p. SR6). Simmons (2001) describes seeing a racist farmer being moved to tears by a story told by a black activist and concludes, "If a radical African American activist can touch the heart of an ultraconservative racist farmer, well, I wanted to know how to do that too" (p. xvi). Stories create those spaces in which people can experience events they might never be able to in their real lives and enable people to see through the eyes of someone drastically different from themselves.

Stories were the original teaching tools, as griots orally passed down lessons from previous generations through stories. Looking over time and across cultures, storytelling is a constant:

> The prevalence of storytelling in human culture may be explained by the use of narrative as a cognitive tool for situated understanding. This *narrative intelligence*—ability to organize experience into narrative form—is central to the cognitive processes employed across a range of experiences, from entertainment to active learning.
>
> (Reidl & Bulitko, 2012, p. 67)

Brown (2000) describes a more modern-day example of stories as learning tools. When Xerox technicians were given manuals, they hardly ever consulted them. Instead, they gleaned their knowledge from stories told by other Xerox technicians. It turns out that what was much more effective than manuals was walkie-talkies (ok, not so modern), which increased learning by 300%. Even more recently, when same-sex marriage was being debated in Massachusetts, politicians credited constituent stories with swaying their opinions, leading to a 50% swing in favor of same-sex marriage (Wangsness and Estes, 2007). We rely on stories to learn and make sense of our surroundings and each other. Even science fiction enables us to gain insights into our current reality by posing extreme worlds that carry out certain ideas. This is being enacted in the present day by women wearing outfits from *The Handmaid's Tale*, a dystopian novel where women are treated as incubators, as a commentary about politics in the United States. Stories enable people to make sense of their world, even if sometimes this is done while exploring the worlds of our imaginations.

Why Are Games So Pedagogically Powerful?

As I write this, my 3-month-old kittens are playfighting at my feet. They are practicing being cats in a safe space and in a safe manner. This is what they choose to do with their time. Anyone around children has probably observed that, left to their own devices, children will play. Even if there are no toys, they will turn an object into a toy. Playing is a natural, instinctive activity that teaches kids, and kittens, about the world. Mayra (2008) defines game-playing as "meaning-making through playful action" (p. 19). Games are a natural extension of play as games are goal-directed play. After all, those who participate in games are called "players."

While I have argued that stories can be powerful learning tools, so can games. Many credit the strategy game of *Weiqi*, or *Go*, as the first learning game as it was used to "train military strategists, chief executives, [and] high-ranking officials" (Jin and Low, 2011, p. 396). The U.S. military greatly advanced videogames as learning tools with *America's Army* (2002), which, through using a first-person point of view and a realistic simulation of a war zone, were not only used as sources of entertainment and recruiting tools but also to train soldiers (Michael & Chen, 2006). My own children spent hours figuring out which plants were best used against which zombies in *Plants vs. Zombies*, learning the strengths and weaknesses of various Pokémon, and devising different strategies to use in chess. Right now I am willing to bet your students are learning a lot from playing videogames, although it may not be what you want them to be learning! While stories enable people to vicariously experience different worlds, games enable people to enact them. Since people get feedback from their gaming experiences and get to try different experiences, games are powerful learning tools, as they offer people opportunities to practice and learn from their mistakes.

It is this cyclical feedback loop of trying something, getting a response, rethinking your strategy based on this response, and trying again that not only leads to learning; it also keeps gameplayers in the "flow" zone. Flow is a state of mind described by

Csikszentmihalyi (1990) in which people are in a mental zone where time has no meaning and reality fades away.[1] He studied how this happens to some people when they work, when they create, and when they play, and what he found is that people get in a flow state when a challenge is perfectly balanced—it's not too easy; otherwise, people get bored, and it's not too hard; otherwise, people get frustrated. As educators, we know this challenge zone as the Zone of Proximal Development, or ZPD (Vygotsky, 1978).

As educators, we also know how hard it is to get a classroom full of students who have varied abilities all perfectly challenged and in the flow zone. Game designers know this too so they have different tactics to achieve this. The most common one is leveling—once a player completes one challenge, they move on to the next harder challenge. As teachers, that is how our curricula are built. However, we have the added challenge of getting everyone to move on at the same time. Many videogames are self-paced and so avoid this problem but others are MMORPGS (Massively Multiplayer Online Role-Playing Games) where players operate in guilds, each person bringing their own abilities to the group. One of the creators of the videogame *EverQuest* explained that they created different classes of players with different sets of abilities so that players would need to rely on each other in order to overcome challenges and thus create a sense of community (McQuaid quoted by Brown, 2008, p. 153). As teachers, we take advantage of this "collective intelligence" (Jenkins, 2009, p. 4) by assigning roles in group work; however, doing so in a way that optimizes everyone's skills can be a challenge, particularly because students can surprise us! I remember one time I configured one of my high school classes into groups only to realize that I had one group with a shy girl among a bunch of rambunctious boys. I almost changed it up, but then I thought, "Let's see what happens." Well, that "shy girl" all of a sudden became this taskmaster who whipped those boys into shape! In this book we will discuss how groups can be a way, but not the only way, to optimize gameplay so students get into the learning zone.

Which Is More Important, Gameplay or Game-story?

As mentioned earlier, in game design, there's been a long-running controversy over which is more important: story (aka narrative) or gameplay (aka ludology). Hard-core gamers claim story is just dressing and that gaming is really about the gameplay itself. However, the popularity of interactive fiction games like *Life Is Strange, Gone Home*, and *A Normal Lost Phone* and the fact that this list keeps expanding defy this maxim.[2] I argue that the narrative versus ludology debate is nonsensical. In fact, even advocating for balancing storytelling and gameplay treats them as mutually exclusive when they are not. For our purposes, the story should be the gameplay, and the gameplay should advance the storyline. A great example of this is the game *It Takes Two*, which is a two-player game about a married couple on the verge of divorce. In order to play the game, the two players have to collaborate because the challenges require both characters to succeed. The core game mechanic, i.e., the repeated action by players in a game, is collaboration—both figuring out what each player needs to do and how to do it together. As the players collaborate to make their way through the game, the story evolves where the couple's love for each other is rekindled.

Despite the claim by some that videogames are only about gameplay, there are videogame historians who claim that the roots of videogames lie in stories, specifically in the stories the Norwegians told themselves to explain their world. While many different contributions and inspirations are attributed to videogame development, including board games and movies, a throughline can be traced back to *Dungeons & Dragons (D&D)*, which some claim was inspired by J.R.R. Tolkien's *Lord of the Rings* book series whose characters' classes and races are derived in large part from Norse mythology. For example, the popular MMORPG *EverQuest* (nicknamed "EverCrack" for its addictive nature) has "Tolkien-inspired sword and sorcery fantasy fiction" (Mayra, 2008, p. 131) as well as *D&D* character classes, combat mechanics, and groups of characters, or guilds, who team up to go on campaigns (Mayra, 2008). These story-based roots have greatly influenced the shape and direction of the videogame industry. Delving into the history of videogames, we see a dual origin of text adventure games such as *Zork* merging with graphics-based games such as *Pong* to create videogames that are immersive storytelling devices where players determine the pace, paths, and endings by making *meaningful* choices—i.e., choices that affect both the story and the gameplay.

Perhaps the ultimate example of the marriage between storytelling and game-playing is *D&D*, a game where players go on a campaign where their successes and failures are determined by strategy, their own traits and tools, dice-throwing, and the Dungeon Master (DM)—i.e., someone who controls the narrative. In fact, *D&D* is perhaps one of the most interdisciplinary learning games out there. Not only does it tap into the English language arts (ELA) elements of characterization, plot development, and so forth, but the game mechanics teach math from basic arithmetic to probability and statistics. With the right content, it could also teach chemistry through potions, physics through combat and other in-game challenges, and biology through healing other characters and animals. Set a *D&D* campaign during a historical event and embed some primary documents, add in some LARPing (live-action role-play), particularly with swordplay for Physical Education, inject some art and music, and you have the whole curricular package! If you are unfamiliar with

D&D, check out https://www.dndbeyond.com/how-to-play-dnd for an introduction and let your students' imaginations soar!

PRACTICE GAME: Interdisciplinary D&D Throughout this book, I am going to have you put together practice games to introduce you to game design. I encourage you to try some of these out with your students.

For this first one, think about a topic in your discipline that has lots of interdisciplinary connections. Now imagine a quest or even a whole *D&D* type campaign where students go on a story-based adventure where they have to use the skills of that topic and the related topics. If you aren't familiar with *D&D* plotlines, you can use this general one: a party of players has to work together to use a map to find various ingredients they need to combine in certain ratios in relation to the weight of the intended target in order to create a sleeping potion to put a monster to sleep so they can obtain a magical artifact the monster has been guarding. As you can see, this involves several different skills—map-reading (social studies), storytelling (ELA), ratios (math), and mixing chemicals (science). In addition, the quests to find the ingredients can require any other number of other skills that you want. Jot down your ideas. Share them with other teachers. Perhaps for that last unit of the school year after standardized testing is done when it is so hard to hold students' attention, you and your fellow teachers could lead groups of students in a cross-curricular *D&D* campaign!

What Are Playable Stories?

This book is about transforming instruction into a game-story so students can *experience* the curriculum, in other words, creating stories that students can play. Adding the "you can play" part to stories gives students ownership over their learning and turns passive learning into active participation. The "you can play" part can range from creating a linear story where students have to complete embedded challenges in order to advance the storyline to a branched narrative where students' choices determine the outcome to emergent stories where students role-play different characters to stories with side quests to mystery-type stories where students have to piece together the narrative from clues to just about anywhere your imagination can take you. What is most important is that students have agency; in other words, their actions determine the story's outcomes.

Oregon Trail, a game where players play as a settler during the westward expansion in the United States, is a good example of a "story you can play." Like a traditional story, it has a beginning and an ending. However, the ending, or goal state, may or may not be reached, thus introducing the fun of uncertainty. There are also multiple ways to get to that ending, which involve decisions made by the players. It is also replayable, making it safe and fun to fail. In fact, a common joke about the *Oregon Trail* is that the player died of dysentery. Most importantly, it allows students to experience history by experimenting with it, although Native Americans pointed out the inaccuracies, which did prompt the makers to consult Native Americans in the remake of *Oregon Trail*. While it is impossible, and not ethical, to have students *physically* experience the trials and tribulations of westward expansion, by *virtually* experiencing it, students are immersed in history instead of just passively observing it through reading a third-person account. Many adults have fond memories of playing *Oregon Trail* in school. Because it was a playable story, they remember it more so than a lecture by the teacher, a paper they wrote, or a discussion in class.

When playing *Oregon Trail*, players make a "series of interesting decisions" (Sid Meier, quoted by Prensky, 2011, p. 272). This definition of a game is reminiscent of the *Choose Your*

Own Adventure books, where readers are faced with decisions throughout. A *Choose Your Own Adventure* model is a good place to start for your first curricular game.[3] Blending the *Choose Your Own Adventure* template where students make decisions that impact the storyline with the type of puzzle-solving featured in the *Encyclopedia Brown* books where the main character puts together clues and uses reasoning to solve mysteries, is a great way to "level up" your game design skills.[4]

> **PRACTICE GAME: Choose Your Own Adventure** If you aren't familiar with *Choose Your Own Adventure* books, check one out from the library and read through it. Then, go to https://www.mission-us.org/ and play one of the games (they are free!). Notice the site has a Teach tab which has curricular resources. Then, think about a momentous event in your field and ask yourself, "What if …" it had turned out differently? For example, what if the British had won the Revolutionary War (would it even be called that?), as one of my students hypothesized in his "Revolution Redo" game. What if humans had decided to use a base 12 system instead of base 10? What if writing had never been invented? Now, take a stack of index cards, write each event and alternate event per card, then write cards following the path of what did happen and cards postulating what might have happened. As you do so, think about all the downstream choices and put a star on each card that involves a decision. Then, imagine what could have happened if a different decision had been made, write out those scenarios, and so on. As you do this, arrange the index cards into a decision tree. Turn the cards over and, for each decision card, put a question mark on the back and for each consequence and other consequence, write on the back of the card one or two words describing that decision (this could be as simple as Yes and No) without giving away the outcome/postu-

lated outcome. Now, ask someone to start at the top of the tree and turn over only one path of cards as they make decisions along the way. You just made your first *Choose Your Own Adventure* curricular game!

You can even create games where students play with story elements. For example, in the game *A Normal Lost Phone*, the player has to piece together the phone owner's story from the photos, texts, dating app (to access it, the player has to figure out the password), and so forth. Much like gossip, where you find out bits and pieces of the story, which are often out of order and sometimes contradictory, the player has to do the mental work of creating connections, making inferences, and resolving contradictions to figure out what is going on. No matter what order the player receives the bits of information, often the challenge is to create a timeline of events. As Epstein (2019) points out, the inferences made when "Jack cheats on Jill; Jill takes a job in another city" (p. 239) are different from reversing the order, "Jill takes a job in another city; Jack cheats on Jill" (p. 240). Epstein (2019) argues that the "more mental work [players] do, the more emotionally engaged they become" (p. 230). Television shows have certainly tapped into this as shows often comprise viewers making and revising hypotheses based on a series of clues, such as the *CSI* franchise. In my first book on game-based teaching, I propose a game where the manuscript of *The Odyssey* is out of order and the player has to figure out what order makes sense based on what Odysseus learns in each episode and applies to the next. Constructing a timeline of events involves analyzing cause and effect, making connections, and synthesizing information. In fact, creating a time line or sequencing anything that needs order could be the "core game mechanic" in your curricular game!

PRACTICE GAME: Mixupitis Choose a story in your field—it might be the story of what led up to the Civil

War, or a fiction story, or the story of how a mathematical concept was used to solve a problem, or a story of how a technology was invented. Now, break that story up into story "beats"—i.e., plot points in the story—and write out (or print out) each story beat on an index card. Make multiple copies of the index cards so you have a full set for each group of students in your class. Shuffle each set and hand them out. Challenge each group to line up in the order they think the story goes. Then each group has to explain to the class why they chose that order. The class then votes on the one they think is correct (voting is optional depending on the dispositions in your class). You then reveal the actual order to see which group came the closest.

If you really want to level up your game-based teaching, you could even try creating emergent gameplay. By emergent, I mean a "bottom-up simulation" with no prescribed storylines, unlike *Choose Your Own Adventure* stories. In other words, a storyworld with a story generator. Think of how the videogame *The Sims* operates. Players inhabit avatars who then go about doing whatever they want to do, creating their own stories, whether that be arguing with a neighbor or rearranging furniture (no one says the stories have to be interesting).[5] If you think about it, *Madlibs* where players fill in blanks based on parts of speech, is a rudimentary story generator. Now you might be thinking, "I don't have the coding skills to program a story generator." Most of us don't, but that shouldn't stop us from learning!

PRACTICE GAME: Madlibs You are going to use a spreadsheet to create a Madlibs game—a game where players fill in words to a story without knowing what the story is. To do so, I'm going to have a set of directions telling you what to do, a set of instructions telling you how to do it, and a visual aid showing you what it looks like. Try using just the directions if you can. *Please note that software tools can change, so these instructions and visuals are as of the writing of this book.*

Directions: Use a spreadsheet to create a madlibs-type story where players input responses to parts of speech or category prompts, which then populate a story by filling in for keywords.

Instructions: Open up a new Google Sheets file. Click on the plus sign in the bottom left-hand corner to create a second sheet. On this second sheet, write out a story that relates to your subject area, with each word in its own cell. Then, take out key words and replace them with their parts of speech or a description of their category (e.g., historical figure, animal, linear equation, astronomical phenomenon). Then, copy and paste each of those categories into column A of the first sheet. Go back to the second sheet and, for the first key word cell, type over what is in it with this: = Sheet1!B1. What you are telling Google Sheets to do is to take whatever item is in cell B1 on the first sheet and put it into that cell in the second sheet. Test it out by typing something in B1 on the first sheet and then going to the second sheet to see if it shows up. Then, type = Sheet1!B2 for the next highlighted cell in sheet 2. Do this for the rest of those cells, adjusting the cell numbers accordingly. Then click the down arrow on the second sheet, select "Hide Sheet," save this and now you have a sponge activity for your class! A sponge activity is one that "absorbs time" that you can have handy if a lesson takes less time than you thought. When students are done filling out their responses, have them go to "View" and select "Hidden Sheets" to see the story they just created.

Visual Aid:

FIGURE 2.1 Madlibs Google Sheets Example.

While the previous practice game taught you some spreadsheet coding, who needs to code when you have students? Since humans are their own natural language processors and can read facial expressions and body language, you can use your students to create emergent stories. Try assigning roles where each character has a different goal. You could even "program" some characters with an algorithm (i.e., every time a character is asked a question, they get increasingly angrier and angrier). Perhaps you want to do *Alice in Wonderland*, where the Queen runs around saying, "Off with their heads," the rabbit is constantly checking his watch and running off, and the Mad Hatter insists on having a tea party. "Where's the drama in that?" you might ask. That is where the DM comes in. In this case, DM stands for "Drama Manager" instead of "Dungeon Master," but it is essentially the same role. It is the DM who is behind the scenes setting up inciting incidents, dramatic choices (which potion should Alice choose?), and delivering consequences. This could be done in a history class (e.g., role-playing the Constitutional Convention), in science class (e.g., role-playing animals in an ecosystem as one of my students did (who says the roles have to be human?)), psychology class (e.g., each student has a random playing card on their backs that they can't see with face cards indicating the popular kids that everyone flocks to and the lower the card, the less popular kids), or any other class with enough imagination.

How Do Different Players Approach Playing Games?

Savvy readers may be thinking that different gameplayers probably enjoy different kinds of games just like different students like different subjects. This might be the crux of the ludology versus narratology dilemma—that it is just a reflection of different player types. For example, students who say they want to find out what happens in the game-story would probably fall more on the narratology end of the spectrum. My students who say they enjoy playing the mini-games I embedded in my latest course would likely fall on the ludology end of the spectrum. I had one student who said what "hooked" her was how my game-based course was "perfectly balanced" between the story and the game challenges. On the other hand, I had another student say he hated the whole thing because he claimed games are for kids and he felt that, as a professional with kids of his own, he shouldn't be wasting his time playing games. That was a hard lesson for me to learn—that not all students will appreciate game-based teaching. When I was a high school English teacher, I had a student who was disappointed she did not get into Advanced Placement English—a class where the teacher was known for being like the stereotypical professors who lecture. She complained that my class was just "games" without any serious learning. You will always have an outlier. What is important is that you check in with your students to refine your game so that as many students as possible are learning and having fun while doing so. If you do have a spoilsport, you can always assign them traditional work that covers the same material. I suspect that when they see everyone else having fun, they will come around.

While there have been various theories about the kinds of players, most fall within Bartle's (1996/2006) four player types: Socializers, Explorers, Achievers, and Killers. Socializers enjoy the social aspects of gaming—playing on a team, talking about a game, or playing games that are more social. Explorers are particularly rewarded when new worlds open up and they find themselves looking in every nook and cranny for new clues or just new sights. Achievers aim to level up, often as quickly as possible, sometimes even "speed running" a game—trying to complete a game in the most time-efficient way possible. Killers like being able to dominate in a game, whether by conquering others or by ruling over a kingdom. Rarely, however, is anyone only one type of player. For example, I witnessed my own child, who tends to be an achiever, act more like a socializer by giving a friend a virtual gift that was perfectly suited for the friend. Even though player types are stereotypes, they can help remind us to incorporate these different aspects into our games just as learner types (visual, auditory, kinesthetic, etc.) remind us to incorporate multiple ways for students to access, process, and present their knowledge in our classrooms—i.e., Universal Design for Learning (UDL). Chris Crawford (2013), who created several serious games about various topics such as the energy crisis, diplomacy, and social interaction, praises teachers for having this ability to reach different types of students: "The act of teaching is mostly a matter of finding an infinite number of ways to communicate an idea. All good teachers have strong second-person insight" (p. 32). A high school physics teacher in one of my research studies captures this type of approach in this quote:

> I constantly try to think about what [students] must be thinking right now.... One of my biggest jobs in class is to listen in all senses of that word so I can understand what

kinds of misconceptions they have or how they're currently thinking to guide them to discover what it's really about.

(Patrick in Jackson, 2007, p. 143)

It is this "second-person insight" that you can tap into to design curricular games that will appeal to your particular students.

One way to do this is to think of the elements of a story—a digital game can be heavy on action/plot (abstract gameplay for achievers), heavy on setting (virtual worlds for explorers), heavy on character development and choices (interactive fiction for socializers), or heavy on conflict (fighting games for killers). Most digital games, however, lie somewhere in the middle, using these different aspects to balance out the game. For example, different character classes can be adept at different skills needed in a game, thus requiring social interaction and achievement in order to unlock new worlds to explore. It is these different combinations that provide a wide range of games, allowing for Bartle's (1996/2006) different player types to derive enjoyment from them. For our purposes, we can design our curricular games to satisfy these different needs. For example, Easter eggs (hidden items in games), secret missions, and side quests appeal to explorers; group play and reflection sessions can appeal to socializers; levels can appeal to achievers; and, as for killers, while we don't want students to dominate each other, you can design a game where the ultimate goal is to defeat the game or even the teacher!

How Can Educators Design Learning Games That Appeal to as Many Player Types as Possible?

I just changed this heading from "all" player types to "as many as possible." Just like you might not be able to make all your students happy, you might not be able to appeal to all player types either. Currently, one of the courses I am teaching is a game-based course that is online and asynchronous. I had one student who made it clear he wanted more interaction with his peers. He's clearly a socializer. I have built in many different ways students can get to know each other and interact in my class, including both text-based and video-based discussion boards and study groups with their own ways of communicating. Despite all this, most students did not take advantage of these opportunities. Results from my midcourse survey explained why: over 75% of the students reported that they don't expect peer interaction in an online asynchronous course with over half saying they prefer to go directly to the professor for help. I am still going to try to foster more peer interaction for those who want it, but it seems most of my students are not craving it. On the other hand, I have had students talk about how leveling up is what keeps them engaged. In fact, one even said they liked that there was a clear "objective" for each level, echoing lesson plan language. These students are clearly achievers. Others talk about loving the storyline and wanting to see where it goes. Those are explorers—always wanting to find out more. While you may not be able to satisfy every type of student player, there are ways to try to reach as many as you can.

Just like every teacher has their own approach to lesson planning, I encourage everyone to develop their own approach to designing curricular games. That being said, having a rough outline to follow at first can be invaluable. That is what this book seeks to do: provide a blueprint that teachers can use to design their first curricular game with enough wiggle room to apply across subjects and grade levels. This book will follow a process based on how elementary teachers explain story design: Somebody Wanted But So Then. In the story snippet above—my introduction to the next class I design—we can see evidence of all these aspects—the "somebody" is the protagonist who developed technological telepathy and "wants" to undo their technology to get it out of dangerous hands, "but" they have to break into the Pentagon to do this, "so" they plan on using their coding skills to hack in and, if successful, "then" they will save democracy.

We will go through each of these elements chapter by chapter, beginning with the *Somebody*—the protagonist of the game, along with the other characters that will come into play. Then, we will explore the *Wanted*, i.e., the goal of that main character, for what is a game, or even a story, without a goal? The But section will introduce conflict since both games and stories are boring if the main character achieves their goal without any obstacles. The *So* involves the skills needed to overcome those obstacles and the *Then* is the final challenge and subsequent win-state, or lose-state, that concludes the game. Since our playable stories will be replayable stories, we want to introduce some uncertainty into our game (some argue that a game is not a game unless it has uncertainty). This might mean an array of endings, like in the *Choose Your Own Adventure* books, or a series of lose-states with only one win-state, or one win-state with the uncertainty of achieving it, or emergent storytelling with no definitive win-state.

While videogames often have large expansive worlds to explore and sometimes even multiple paths to winning, Dille and Platten (2007), who co-wrote the *Chronicles of Riddick* videogame, observe that "the reality of story-driven games is that you usually have an optimal path: the spine of the game where the main action and events take place" (p. 50). For our educational purposes, linear games, or at least ones with a "golden path," work well because we can guarantee all students get the core material while also implementing Gee's (2007) notion of having a series of "well-ordered problems" (p. 35). Schrier (2007) found that linear gameplay worked better for her students because they found it more "goal-oriented" (p. 264) and felt more secure knowing they were on the right path. My current coding class follows a linear storyline where students have to complete challenges that increase in difficulty in order to unlock the next story segment.

Keep in mind our purpose is for students to learn, unlike the videogame industry whose goal is to make money.

While creating a game designed to be played once can work well for our purposes, there are also strong arguments for replayability, particularly when it serves a pedagogical purpose. For example, you might want to have a *Choose Your Own Adventure* style game based on *The Outsiders*, as one of my students did, or, really, any other novel, historical event, scientific discovery, etc., where students can play through as different characters. Or a physical game similar to *Red Rover* where students play different parts of the immune system, as another one of my students designed. Or, you might want to have students replay a game multiple times with different conditions to teach students how to distinguish between two or more instances of something, for example, different manifestations of a disease.

Replayability works well when you want to teach students how to apply a set of skills to a range of situations. For example, one of the mini-games in my English Methods class involves students role-playing a conference with a parent whose child has plagiarized. I have students line up, and for the first role-play, I play the parent. Once the student role-playing the teacher succeeds by mollifying the parent, they then become the parent and the next student in line the teacher. However, if the parent threatens to go to the principal, the student has to go to the back of the line and try again. When students role-play the parent, they pick an index card out of a hat with a set of instructions so that every scenario is different. These instructions include situations like the parent accuses the teacher of being racist, or threatens to take the teacher to court, or threatens to have them fired, or threatens to beat their own child, or inadvertently admits to writing the paper themselves, or doesn't know what plagiarism is, or claims that every student does it. This mini-game works well because it combines chance (you don't know what the scenario is going to be) with skill (the instructions for the parent include what is required to convince them, such as providing evidence).

Having the same gameplay in multiple contexts also helps students move concrete knowledge to abstract rules, as students have to figure out what works in all or almost all situations and what is contextual (Bransford et al., 2000). One of the advantages of playing games in a classroom setting is that you can save time by having students or small groups of students play through the game from different perspectives or scenarios and use a debriefing session to compare those experiences. Using replayability in these ways creates conditional knowledge—knowing when to apply different sets of information and skills.

One of the pedagogical advantages of story-based games is that, when done well, learners *pull* information in order to figure out the challenges instead of having information *pushed* onto them. For example, one of my students designed a *Choose Your Own Adventure*–type game where the players play as a runaway slave. One of the choices was whether or not to go to a "contraband camp." I must admit I had to "pull" that information by looking up the meaning when I played, which gave me much more ownership over my learning than if I had passively heard it in a lecture or read the definition in a book. According to the screenwriter Alex Epstein (2019), "Pushing information at the audience pushes them away" (p. 231), which, if you think about it, is what we do as educators when we lecture our students. He suggests using the following mechanics to get players to want to find out more: "translucent lies, absences, mysteries, and inconsistencies" (p. 231) because they get players to ask questions and want to seek out answers. For example, in the videogame *Peace Island*, there are remnants of humans but no humans (but there are lots of cats!). "Mysteries of History" are perfect for this: What did happen to the settlers at the Lost Colony? Was there more than one shooter in JFK's assassination? Did FDR have advanced knowledge of Pearl Harbor but let it happen anyway so the United States would have a reason to go to war? Even just using content-based terms in player choices can lead to students actively pulling information instead of pushing it onto them.

When players don't get fed answers, then they have to use their powers of interpretation to figure them out. It is the cycle of not knowing (curiosity) and the knowing (figuring something out) that makes interpretation pleasurable.

How Can You Get Started with This Process?

The following chapters are going to go into more detail about each of the steps of this process. You will likely find that you will employ a two-stage iterative design process. The first stage involves moving back and forth between the macro and the micro—something you likely do when you initially design a brand-new unit plan: start with the big picture and then fill in the details. As you do, there are probably times you mentally tweak the big picture as the details reveal a slightly different direction to go in, and you discard some details and seek out others that better fit the overarching goal. This is the iterative—or back-and-forth—part of the design process. The second stage of iterative design is refining your curricular game, similar to the feedback loop you use to improve your lesson plans after you teach them or sometimes even as you teach them. When you teach, you find out what works with your students and what doesn't and revise accordingly. In videogame design, this process is called playtesting. For our purposes, playtesting will start before you teach using your curricular game and continue as you get feedback from implementing it and from debriefing sessions. As teachers, we really have the ideal playtesting situation as we get new groups of playtesters every time we teach a class, allowing us to make our revisions between terms or sometimes even between earlier classes and classes later in the day. But, for now, let's focus on getting a rough outline of the big picture.

Our game-story, like almost all stories, will follow the Somebody Wanted But So Then story structure. In other words, the main character (Somebody), in our case the player, has a goal

(Wanted); however (But) there is an impediment to reaching that goal. In order to overcome that obstacle or obstacles, the player needs to take some actions (So) and, upon successful completion, the resolution (Then) is reached.

> **ACTION ITEM:** Take at least three games you played (these could be from the new games you played for chapter one) and make a chart identifying the Somebody, Wanted, But, So, and Then of each of the games. Here is an example: Somebody = Pac-Man, a round head with a chomping mouth, Wanted to clear a maze of dots But there are ghosts that harm him So he actively avoids the ghosts while trying to eat all the dots in the most efficient way possible Then, when he completes a level, he moves on to a more difficult maze. Look across the elements you identified for the games. Do you see any patterns?

Once you have completed the action item above, look through the different elements of Somebodies, Wanteds, Buts, Sos, and Thens to determine which of these elements matches with what you would label learning objectives in lesson plans. In other words, what the students do in the Procedures section. This is the core game mechanic—the skill that players improve upon throughout the game. That's right! It is the "So" of the game. To figure out the rough outline of your game-story, start there, in the middle, with the "So." Keep in mind that while the details may change, the So is the "core game mechanic"—i.e., the repeated action you want players to take. In other words, the end of this sentence when you write your lesson plans: "Students will be able to …" or, for objectives written from the point of view of students, the endings of the "I can …" statements. For now, choose the unit you want to turn into a game; look at the major unit goal and across the objectives of the lesson plans. What is the primary skill that students are improving upon throughout the unit in order to achieve the unit goal? Maybe it's identifying bias in primary sources, or solving linear functions, or making inferences based on foreshadowing, or completing a Punnett square. Whatever it is, that is your "So." When you identify this skill, make it an action verb and avoid the word "understand." While Wiggins and McTighe (1998) in *Understanding by Design* talk about "enduring understandings," these are the bigger picture of what you want to stay with students. How these enduring understandings are achieved needs to be more specific than using the word "understand," after all, the word "understand" has so many different meanings in the English language (comprehend, empathize, interpret, agree, and so forth).

Go ahead and start thinking about who (or what) might be using that skill in order to overcome an obstacle to an overarching goal. Keep these flexible for now while the "So" is fixed—that is, unless you decide to start over and create a different game for a different topic. When you get to the "So" chapter, you'll think more about how that will happen, but for now, in your Design Document (the videogame designer equivalent of a unit plan), write down your core game mechanic as that skill that you identified. Don't worry about whether or not you can create a photo-realistic videogame that will rival the *Legend of Zelda* franchise. As Kurt Squire (2011) found out, "Kids compared [*Supercharged!*— the educational videogame Squire helped create] to 'what they did at school' rather than 'the games they played at home'" (p. 96). This has been my experience as well. For example, one of my students said my class was "unlike" any other course they had taken. Notice that student did not compare my course to a game but rather compared my course to their other courses.

You may have noticed that this chapter had you create several games on the spot. One of the issues I found in teaching with my first book on game design is that I had students go slowly through the process of creating one epic game. Students who took the course were eager to get started and I could tell they found the process overly laborious. My aim for this book is to get my readers to create lots of games while also laying out a process for a more in-depth game. This mirrors the evolution of game design. Bond (2018) explains how game designers have moved from an overreliance on design documents (think unit plans) to rapid prototyping (think teaching on the fly), where a designer aims to get a workable game out as quickly as possible (think of this as a rough draft) so they can playtest it. These workable games are usually paper prototypes because they are so quick and easy to create and to make changes to. Game designers often use hex paper (think of a paper with a drawing of a beehive) because it allows for movement in six different directions (you could even use masking tape to "draw" this out on your classroom floor), index cards to list player choices, dice as a randomizer tool (note that for a 6-sided die, each number has the same probability but, if you roll 2 six-sided dice, the probability forms a bell curve), and pipe cleaners shaped into objects and/or creatures. The initial games are usually turn-based even if the final gameplay is not going to be. This allows game designers to "respond to change" instead of "following a plan" (Bond, 2018, p. 224). As teachers, we know that flexibility is the number one characteristic teachers need in order to survive because we never know what students are going to do or say! Flexibility is also key in game design.

> **PRACTICE GAME:** Get a stack of colored index cards. On one color, write several different "Somebodies"—various characters (e.g., zombie, little girl, Abraham Lincoln, rabbit). On another, different "Wanteds"—various goals (e.g., figure out who killed their parents, slay the monster terrorizing the town, find a hidden treasure). On a third, different "Buts"—various obstacles (e.g., a hurricane, more monsters, a character with the opposite goal). Shuffle the cards by color. Choose one from each stack. And then think of the "So," the repeated skill, that would go along with the other elements to come up with a game-story. Now, ask *ChatGPT* or some other artificial

intelligence (AI) tool to create a game-story with those elements. Compare your game-story to the AI one. In this work, it is fine to use AI to help you! Just remember, though, to always have a human in the loop by reviewing and adjusting the output.[6]

Conclusion

To demonstrate the difference between traditional teaching and game-based teaching, I am going to use a word problem from a software tutoring program: "Suppose a runner is running in a straight line at a constant speed and the runner throws a pumpkin straight up. Where will the pumpkin land? Explain your answer" (Van Eck, 2007, p. 292). This is an isolated problem that not only does not motivate students to solve it, but it has no context in which it makes sense. Instead, I suggest this much more fun version:

> "You are running away from the zombies that are chasing you. They are about 20 feet behind you and running at your same pace—5 miles per hour. In your hands is a grenade that will decimate them if you can launch it and hit them before they decimate you. Should you throw the grenade at a 45-degree angle in front of you, straight up, or at a 45-degree angle behind you?"

Reading this, you are motivated to figure out the answer because your survival instincts kick in. As Hirumi and Stapleton (2008) point out, "Stories evoke emotional investment in gameplay. It answers the question, 'Why should I care?'" (p. 148). My students affirmed this in their feedback on my game-based courses when they talked about wanting to level up so they could find out what happens in the story. Getting students to care about the curriculum creates motivation, investment, and ownership over their learning—all those intangibles that help ensure long-term learning, i.e., enduring understandings, which is much more important than short-term cramming for a test just to get an A.

Chapter 2 Worksheet: Design Document Rough Draft

Directions: Fill out the following chart with as much, or as little, detail as you want at this point. Do not feel wed to anything you write. This is just a place for you to explore some initial ideas. Plan on returning to this and making changes throughout the game design process.

	Initial Ideas	Possible Alternatives
Working Title		
Topic		
Core Game Mechanic (the "So" or SWBAT[a] skill)		
Target Audience (Grade level, class title, background info on students, player types if known)		
Main Character/Player Avatar (the Somebody)		
Backstory		
Main Character's Goal (the Wanted)		
Obstacles (the Buts)		
Game-Story Structure (D&D, *Choose Your Own Adventure*, linear series of "well-ordered problems," emergent, etc.)		

	Initial Ideas	Possible Alternatives
Game Summary		
Feedback (Ask former and current students if they've ever played a game that touches on this topic; ask them how they would design a game about the topic; run your ideas by them to get their input)		

[a] Students will be able to …

Notes

1. Recently, my twins couldn't let go of an argument they were having, so I took them rock climbing. There's nothing like trying to survive that helps people get into the flow zone where day-to-day concerns fade away.
2. I just played a very intense, powerful interactive fiction game called *Tell Me Why*, which naturally embeds in the storyline lessons about Alaskan culture, Tlingit practices, being trans, and the queer community.
3. *MissionUS* has a series of historical games based on the *Choose Your Own Adventure* model of gameplay and they are free!
4. The website http://escapeif.com has several examples in this vein (mostly for primary grades), as well as advice and worksheets.
5. Johnson (2005) tells of his 7-year-old nephew suggesting he "lower his industrial tax rates" (p. 32) to solve a problem he was having in *SimCity*, which is a great example of the power of learning by doing.

6. My father was a notoriously bad speller, and he knew it, so he trusted the computer more than himself, resulting in him printing up 800 copies of a catalogue that said, "First come, first severed."

References

Bartle, R. (1996/2006). Hearts, clubs, diamonds, spades: Players who suit MUDs. In K. Salen and E. Zimmerman (Eds.), *The game designer reader: A rules of play anthology* (pp. 754–787) Cambridge, MA: MIT Press.

Bond, J. (2018). *Introduction to game design, prototyping, and development*. Upper Saddle River, NJ: Addison-Wesley.

Bransford, J., Brown, A., & Cocking, R. (2000). *How people learn: Brain, mind, experience, and school*. Washington, DC: National Academies Press.

Brown, H. (2008). *Videogames and education*. Armonk, NY: M.E. Sharpe.

Brown, J. S. (2000, March/April). Growing up digital: How the web changes work, education, and the ways people learn. *Change: The Magazine of Higher Learning, 32*(2), 10–20.

Crawford, C. (2013). *On interactive storytelling*. Berkeley, CA: New Riders.

Csikszentmihalyi, M. (1990). *Flow: The psychology of optimal experience*. New York: Harper & Row.

Dille, F. & Platten, J. S. (2007). *The Ultimate guide to videogame writing and design*. New York, NY: Lone Eagle Publishing Company.

Epstein, A. (2019). Dirty procedural storytelling in *We Happy Few*. In T. Short & T. Adams (Eds.), *Procedural storytelling in game design* (pp. 227–240). Boca Raton, FL: CRC Press.

Gee, J.P. (2007). *Good videogames + good learning: Collected essays on videogames, learning, and literacy*. New York: Peter Lang.

Hirumi, A. & Stapleton, C. (2008). Applying pedagogy during game development to enhance game-based learning. In C. T. Miller (Ed.), *Games: Purpose and potential in education* (pp. 127–162). New York: Springer.

Jackson, J. (2007). *Unmasking identities: An exploration of the lives of gay and lesbian teachers*. Lanham, MD: Lexington Books.

Jenkins, H. (2009). *Confronting the challenges of a participatory culture: Media education for the 21st century*. Cambridge, MA: MIT Press.

Jin, P. and Low, R. (2011). Implications of game use for explicit instruction. In S. Tobias & J.D. Fletcher (Eds.), *Computer games and instruction* (pp. 395–416). Charlotte, NC: Information Age Publishers.

Johnson, S. (2005). *Everything bad is good for you: How today's popular culture is actually making us smarter*. New York: Riverhead Books.

Kellinger, J. (2022). *Coding for Non-Coders*. Course taught in the College of Education and Human Development at UMass Boston, Fall '22-present.

Mayra, F. (2008). *An introduction to game studies*. Thousand Oaks, CA: Sage.

Michael, D. & Chen, S. (2006). *Serious games: Games that educate, train, and inform*. Boston, MA: Thomson.

Paul, A. M. (2012, March 17). Your brain on fiction. *New York Times*, p. SR6.

Prensky, M. (2011). Comments on research comparing games to other instructional methods. In S. Tobias and J. D. Fletcher (Eds.), *Computer games and instruction* (pp. 251–280). Charlotte, NC: Information Age Publishers.

Reidl, M. & Bulitko, V. (2012). Interactive narrative: An intelligent systems approach. *AI Magazine, 34*(1), 67–77.

Schrier, K. (2007). Reliving history with 'Reliving the Revolution': Designing augmented reality games to teach the critical thinking of history. In D. Gibson, C. Aldrich, & M. Prensky (Eds.), *Games and simulations in online learning: Research and development frameworks* (pp. 250–269). Hershey, PA: Information Science Publishing.

Simmons, A. (2001). *The story factor: Inspiration, influence, and persuasion through the art of storytelling*. New York: Basic Books.

Squire, K. (2011). *Videogames and learning: Teaching and participatory culture in the digital age*. NY: Teachers College Press.

Van Eck, R. (2007). Building artificially intelligent learning games. In D. Gibson, C. Aldrich, & M. Prensky (Eds.), *Games and simulations in online learning: Research and development frameworks* (pp. 271–307). Hershey, PA: Information Science Publishing.

Vygotsky, L. (1978). *Mind in society*. Cambridge, MA: Harvard University Press.

Wangsness, L. & Estes, A. (2007, June 15). Personal stories changed minds. *Boston Globe*.

Wiggins, G. & McTighe, J. (1998). *Understanding by design*. Alexandria, VA: ASCD.

3

Creating the Characters (Somebody)

> *You have invented a way to view the Earth's interior!* ***Your Geology Glasses*** *allow the user to see right through layers of dirt, rock, and magma, all the way to the center of the Earth!* ***You*** *can adjust your Geology Glasses to see features that are closer to the surface or deeper underneath.* ***You****'re sure this is going to be a ground-breaking technology when it hits the market!* ***You*** *just have to convince people about the usefulness of it.*
>
> (Molly Travers, *Volcano Vision*, 2022, bolding is my own)

The quote comes from the beginning of a curricular game designed by one of my students. When creating game-stories, the protagonist *is* the student/player, so your game-story should be written in second person, like in the excerpt. A second-person story? Remember, this is a game-story, just like the *Choose Your Own Adventure* books are written in second person as well. As Richter and Livingstone (2011) point out, in videogames players "do not think of themselves controlling a character on screen—but think of being that character and carrying out the avatar's actions themselves" (p. 109).[1] Because your students will be playing your story, you should begin your game-story with "You." The essential difference between a character in a story and a character in a game-story is agency. Sylvester (2013) defines agency as "the ability to make decisions and take meaningful actions that affect the game world" (p. 101). This includes

DOI: 10.4324/9781003584308-3

linear game-stories where the player's actions impact pacing, the revelation of rewards, gathering information, and so forth. Swan (2010) asserts that "the notion of agency...is at the heart of engagement and immersion" (p. 118). Placing students as the "you" in the game is what enables your students to have agency and therefore *experience* the curriculum.

Just like the word "understand" is vague because there are so many different types of understanding, so is the word "experience." You can physically experience something. You can mentally experience something. You can cognitively experience something. You can emotionally experience something. Games with characters and stories have the potential to tap into all these different types of "experiencing." Dille and Platten (2007) point out that "characters and story give the player something they can invest in emotionally" (p. ix). Sylvester (2013) describes games as "systems for generating experiences" (p. 305). I would argue that characters in game-stories turn games into "systems for generating empathy" as well. As teachers, we know the power of evoking empathy. The following quotes come from K–12 teachers' lesson plans from one of my research studies:

- "What does it feel like to be invaded?"
- "What do you think it was like back then?"
- "Imagine if you were just minding your own business and people came and took over your land. How would you feel?"

(Jackson, 2007, p. 143)

As you can see, these teachers have their students view the world from the perspectives of others, thus engendering empathy. One of these teachers talked about how important empathy is:

[E]mpathy I think is I would say the most powerful human tool. We don't spend enough time either talking

> about it or working on it and, if we all had more empathy, I think we would all not step on each other's toes and hurt each other as much.
>
> (Patrick in Jackson, 2007, p. 144)

This has been borne out in studies about empathy reducing bullying (Blanchard, 2007). Because seeing the world from another person's point of view challenges assumptions, empathy can be used to counter stereotypes.

Rusch (2017) explains how experiences evoke empathy:

> Games enable embodied experiences—meaning that, in a game, we learn by doing and by acting upon the gameworld and seeing the consequences of our actions just like in real life (see Gee 2003). [Games] are thus particularly well suited to evoke empathy, and to engage in perspective taking, because they do not just *show* aspects of someone else's life; they also allow the player to walk in someone else's shoes, *experiencing* life from their perspective.
>
> (p. xx)

Rusch (2017) continues by demonstrating how videogames can create "embodied experiences" that emulate our inner worlds by describing how swinging, letting go, and catching the next rope in a game mimics feelings of transition—the risk of letting go of the old, the suspense of not knowing if you will be successful in your new choice, and the satisfaction of success. I used this idea of "embodied experience" when creating a mini-game as part of my coding game-story where the player has to "grasp" onto consciousness in order to come out of a stupor. I thought about how, when I am in a half-asleep/half-awake state, whether I focus on the moments I am more asleep or the moments I am more awake determines if I wake up or not. In my mini-game, players have to click on the backdrop when it is the most clear; otherwise, they lose consciousness. If players don't regain consciousness in time, or if they reach the unconscious end of the scale, they don't wake up. Of course, players get a chance to retry as many times as they need to succeed. In this way, I designed the game to emulate regaining consciousness, furthering the player's identification with the playable character.

Rusch (2017) points to figures of speech as being fruitful sources of inspiration for creating moments of experiential embodiment in games by providing examples such as "walking on eggshells," "being someone's punching[bag]," "walking on a tightrope," and "having your back against a wall" (p. 74) as well as common metaphors (what she calls "experiential metaphors") such as climbing ladders as representing improvement, going underground as discovering secrets, and cleaning as getting rid of what is undesirable (pp. 49–52). She cites *Angry Birds*, a videogame where birds hurl rocks at the pigs who stole their eggs, as an example of experientially emulating vengeance: pulling back the slingshot is the "build-up of anger," releasing it is the "momentary loss of control" as the consequences of the act of vengeance is unknown, and success allows the player to revel in the destruction their action wreaked (pp. 80–82). Using "you" in our game-stories allows our students to put themselves in someone, or something, else's shoes and experience the world as they do, which is one of the most powerful learning experiences people can have.

When designing your game, keep in mind that the "you" does not need to be human. Lee Sheldon (2014) claims that people read stories for three reasons: "1) Take me to a place I have never been. 2) Make me into someone I could never be. 3) Let me do things I could never do." (p. 11). Having the playable character be a nonhuman object can satisfy all three of these desires. Students in my *Introduction to Game-based Teaching* class have created games where their students are water droplets going through the water cycle, animals in an ecosystem having to deal with natural disasters, and even parts of the immune system. In fact, empathizing with objects is common in our lives. For example, when parking a car, we often say, "I don't think I can fit in there" (Schell, 2008, p. 312) when actually it is the car that cannot fit. Experts often explain their thinking from nonhuman perspectives: "Orville Wright pretend[ed] to be a buzzard gliding over the sand dunes and Albert Einstein imagin[ed] himself to be a photon speeding over the earth" (Jenkins, 2009, p. 52). I saw this in K–12 teachers who said things like, "If you're carbon and you're in this environment with all these other atoms, how are you going to feel? What are your needs going to be?" (Jackson, 2007, p. 143). When you are considering who the "you" will be in your game-story, do not limit yourself to human protagonists or even animal protagonists. Having students "be" objects in a system is a powerful way for them to think about how that system operates.

Who Is the "You"?

Depending on your game-story, you may want the protagonist to have an elaborate backstory or none at all. In fact, the point of the game could be to figure out the player's backstory. Certainly there have been many "amnesia" movies and games that do just this. If you do have a backstory, Rabin (2009) recommends spreading out the backstory throughout the gameplay; otherwise, the player will get all this information before they even care about the playable character and it will be like, "[Y]our Aunt Myrtle dron[ing] on and on about a childhood friend" (p. 150). Spreading out the information also creates suspense. In fact, starting out "in media res"—in the middle of the action—can really create suspense! Think of it like a "hook" you might create for a class lesson. Imagine if your game starts off with the main character being fired upon by pirates or being chased by flying monkeys. That will certainly raise questions that students will want to answer! For example, in my coding class where students start off handcuffed and gagged with intruders rifling through their office, I could tell them right away what the thieves are trying to steal, but instead I have the playable character, who is woozy from being knocked out by the intruders, try and fail to remember. Writing the game-story this way leads my students to wonder, "What could be so important that thieves would want to steal it" Meanwhile, I drop hints, what us English teachers call foreshadowing, about the invention of mentally being able to program a robot. For example, when the "you" remembers that their robot's name is Sparky, the text says, "You feel like Sparky is a good friend, or even closer. Almost like the two of you are on the same wavelength. 'Good friend?' you think. 'What is wrong with me? It's a bunch of metal!'" Even though the player probably won't make the connection at this point, when they do find out, they realize that the text has been leading them to that conclusion all along, and they get that combination "aha/duh" moment of thinking, "Of course! I should have known that all along." Parsing out the story, particularly after the player achieves something, gives the player the reward of unlocking more of the story. Rabin (2009) also recommends indirectly conveying the backstory through the setting, signs, sounds, finding items such as part of a newspaper or a journal, stumbling across a radio and listening to a broadcast, or having non-playable characters (NPCs) say things in context that reveal more of the story. By "showing" instead of "telling," "the player learns about the backstory actively and while engaged, instead of passively absorbing it" (p. 150). Prensky (2002) warns that "gamers hate telling" (p. 10). Using environmental cues, NPCs, foreshadowing, and any other indirect means of conveying the backstory immerses the player instead of breaking the flow.

However, Jesse Schell (2008), who created *Toontown Online*, argues that the less detail about the playable character, the better so that each individual player can project themselves onto that playable character and imagine themselves as that character in the game because then nothing contradicts how they define themselves. Lots of first-person shooter games are like this, where the person playing sees what their avatar sees but does not see themselves. I have found, though, that there does not need to be an exact match. In fact, when my twins were 2, they would point at their Miis (Wii avatars) and say, "That's me," or "That's my brother," even when the Miis looked nothing like them. When given the opportunity to design their own avatars, people range from choosing features that resemble themselves, choosing features that create an avatar that looks like who they want to be,[2] and choosing features that create something fantastical, such as a dragon head on a lion's body. Often, this depends on the purpose of the game:

> If the goal of your game is personal transformation such as losing weight, you probably want to have your students choose or define their own avatar so they can be inspired by a "mini-me." However, if your goal is to learn concepts or skills, you might want to choose the avatar for them or create a "blank slate" avatar. If the goal is for students to experience a different perspective or different perspectives, the character they embody should have different experiences than they have had.
> (Kellinger, 2017, p. 80)

I do want to emphasize the liberatory power of "being" someone else, particularly for teenagers who are in Erikson's (1950) identity exploration phase. I remember when I was a college student, I was assigned to write a paper from the perspective of a famous feminist. Because I was writing it as if I were another person, writing that paper allowed me to explore lines of thinking that

I had not been willing to consider previously. Think carefully about what you want to achieve with your game when deciding how to craft the playable character.

Having the playable character be a blank slate allows the player to define the character's personality by making active choices as that character. Short (2019) defines personality as "what we do and why we do it" (p. 271). By this definition, player choices shape the personality of the playable character. That being said, you may have reason to create a playable character with certain personality traits, or the playable character may come with personality traits—for example, if students are playing as a historical or literary figure. Crawford (2013) offers a list of personality traits that imply certain actions, reactions, and responses: "Adventurous-Cautious; Disciplined-Sloppy; Sociable-Solitary; Friendly-Unfriendly; Anxious-Confident; ... Gullible-Suspicious; Willful-Pliant; Nice-Nasty; Honest-False; ... Loquacious-Taciturn; Generous-Greedy; Chaste-Licentious; Humble-Proud; Ascetic-Sensual; Smart-Stupid" (pp. 200–203). Remember that your students will be embodying the playable character so you want to choose traits that students would want to be and save the "anxious, stupid, sloppy, licentious" characteristics for the other characters in your game-story. That being said, assigning a virtue and a vice can help humanize the main character and determine the rewards and punishments you use in a game. I am currently watching a television show where the main character keeps making mistakes; however, because she is so likable and well-meaning, you feel sympathy for her instead of aversion. Dille and Platten (2007) point out, "If people care about your characters, they will forgive a lot" (p. 31). Having the playable character be likable despite, or sometimes even because, of their flaws can go a long way to pulling students into character.

Even though you might want to have the playable character have a vice, you do want them to be a hero, so it works well to make them special in some way. A common construct in stories and games is to have the main character be "the Chosen One." In fact, some stories even use this kind of language, such as Neo in *The Matrix* being called "the one" and Harry Potter "the Chosen One." Imbuing the main character with a special ability, such as *Spider-Man* being able to scale walls and swing from his web, not only makes the player feel special but also allows for certain gameplay actions. On the other hand, having an ordinary person who has done something extraordinary, such as inventing geology glasses like in the excerpt at the beginning of this chapter or technological telepathy like in the coding course I have described in this book, holds out the possibility that ordinary students could themselves be special. These special abilities or tools should enable the player to perform the core game mechanic—i.e., the repeated skill that the player improves upon throughout the game, aka the learning objective.

As you may remember from English class, while most other characters remain static, the main character should be dynamic. So perhaps the main character does start off as anxious, but, over the course of the game as they achieve more and more success, they become more confident. Characters changing personalities is compelling. Saltsman (2019) suggests randomly choosing past and present "micro-stories" to make "couplets" that are oxymorons, such as, "Hated camping as a kid. Sleeps under the stars now," OR "Tortured squirrels when younger. Hoping to find a dog [as a companion]" (Saltsman, 2019, p. 301) because they create suspense, as readers want to find out what made the difference.

> **ACTION ITEM:** Try your hand at creating some opposite past and present couplets.

Make sure that any change in character is both gradual enough and substantiated through the game-story, otherwise it will feel out of character. As the character's personality changes throughout the game-story, you can signify this change by changing the looks of the avatar through different clothes, adding accessories, and improving inventory items. This kind of "badging" has meaning as it reflects changes in character due to achievements in the game. Remember that even a single prop, such as an eye patch signifying a pirate, can conjure up a whole host of "evoked narratives" (Mateas and Stern, 2006, p. 673), such as, for pirates, operating outside the law. Having a closetful of costumes and props in your classroom can go a long way toward creating immersive characters.

Regardless of a strong personality, some suggested personality traits, or a player-constructed personality, you want your students to be able to identify with the character they are playing in your game-story. Sylvester (2013) describes the two-factor theory of emotion: that all physiological arousal is the same (increased heart rate, sweaty palms, etc.), but we label it with different emotions depending on the context (pp. 40–42). He explains that

> to create an experience that mirrors that of a character, [videogame designers] construct it out of three parts. First, we create flow to strip the real world out of the player's mind. Second, we create an arousal state using threats and challenges in the game mechanics. Finally, we use the fiction layer to label the player's arousal to match the character's feelings.
>
> (p. 42)

One way to induce this arousal is to create stress by putting a time crunch on a challenge. However, just like too much challenge leads to frustration, too much stress leads to cognitive impairment. How I handle that dilemma in the "big boss battle," or final challenge where all skills are brought to bear, in my coding class is to limit students to 60 seconds to figure out how to surround the thieves in order to delay the thieves long enough for the police to arrive; however, students can try to do this minute-long test as many times as they need to in order to be successful.

Because your students become the playable character, you need to choose the playable character carefully. My advice is that everyone loves zombies, but no one wants to be a Nazi. Let me amend that. Everyone loves stories about zombies, whether they are a zombie themselves or are fighting zombies. I came to this conclusion one day when my own kids were playing *Plants versus Zombies*, and I was playing a game called *Night of the Living Debt* where the player learns financial literacy by playing a zombie who has to learn how to manage their money in the zombie world. Inspired by these games, I created my own game in *Scratch*, a free block-based programming language, for my students studying to become teachers called *Zombie School* where they are student teachers who go to Zombie University where the slogan is "We teach the best brains," which is later vandalized and turned into "We eat the best brains." As zombie student teachers, they need to help prepare zombie kids to be successful in the upcoming zombie apocalypse. When the students they are teaching become overwhelmed, the student teachers need to give students a brain break, otherwise known as snack time. I'm not the only educator game designer who has capitalized on the zombie theme. I had one student create a game called *The Antidote*, where players have to formulate an antidote to zombie bites and sell it, and another called *Dead Run* where students had to outrun zombies by learning lessons about long-distance running techniques. As you can see, you can have a lot of fun when your students play as zombies or against zombies. Imagine having to run a presidential campaign that wins over the zombies that have taken over the world or using geometry to figure out the correct positioning and trajectory to lob bombs to defeat the zombies chasing you. You don't have to use a zombie story for your game-story, but zombies are both appalling and appealing, so keep them in mind for future games. You might also want to think about other creatures that are appealing, such as kittens and puppies, for your students to be. Characters can go a long way in creating games that people want to play.

On the other hand, no one wants to be a Nazi. This is general advice extrapolated to mean that you don't want to design a game-story where students have to play someone who is an awful person. In one of my games, I planted an Easter egg, a just-for-fun item that players can discover by clicking on the right place, where, if players clicked on the mirror in the room, they would see a reflection of themselves. Initially, I had a cartoon of Michael Jackson flashing a peace sign. Then, the Michael Jackson documentary came out that detailed the horrific things he did, and I realized no one wants to be Michael Jackson, so I changed it to an animation of Jim Parsons, the actor who plays Sheldon in *The Big Bang Theory*. While it may be tempting to have students play different roles in a historical time period, there are some roles that would be insensitive or even traumatizing for students to play. In those cases, you could have the teacher play that role or an NPC be that role, or perhaps that event is not something you want to turn into a game because it is so horrific that making it into a game would trivialize it.

Keep in mind that your game-story does not need to have just one main character that each student plays individually. You can have the whole class play as the main character, making decisions together and engaging in engrossing discussions about what to do next and why. Having a PowerPoint or Google Slideshow displayed on the front wall or, better yet, have four projectors on all four walls to really immerse the class (e.g., if the setting is in the woods, you could have three walls showing trees and the fourth at the front of the room showing a path through the woods with branching forks) can really help set the scene. You can have small groups play through as the main character while you go from group to group observing, listening in, and dropping hints.[3] Or you can have each student roleplay a different character, such as in the game one of my students created, where the playable characters are all from different social classes during the Black Plague. However you do it, remember to frame your game-story in second person to make it clear that students *are* their character.

What about Other Characters?

While you could have a game-story where you have just the protagonist and no other characters, most stories involve more than one character. In video games, characters that are not being controlled by the player are called NPCs. Unlike avatars, which are videogame characters controlled by a human being, NPCs are agents, videogame characters controlled by computer programming. Just like there are stock characters in books, on television shows, and in the movies, there are stock characters in videogames for a good reason. They serve a purpose. This purpose might be as an enemy's henchman, or as a red herring, or as a co-conspirator. The role of NPCs is to move the plot along—even if sometimes moving the plot along means derailing the plot to present a challenge or decision for the player. If an NPC does not add to the gameplay in some way, then that NPC is extraneous and should be eliminated. In almost all games, the player is the hero. You can usually place NPCs into one of three categories (or sometimes, into two or three categories at the same time) in relation to the hero: the helpers, the hinderers, and the helped (Kellinger, 2017).

Helpers tend to be mentors, sidekicks, or even messengers bringing more information. Their role is to dole out advice, suggestions, hints, and guidance. However, there is a problem with helpers. If they know what to do, why aren't they doing it themselves? I call this the Dumbledore problem, as in why didn't Dumbledore, if he knew so much, either tell Harry Potter what to do or do it himself in the Harry Potter series? I suspect that the answer to that question, if you were to ask Dumbledore himself, is that he knew that Harry would only learn these lessons if Harry discovered the answers himself. That is one tactic.

Other approaches can be that the expert helper is physically constrained in some way (disabled, in jail, in another dimension, old, lost their magic touch, forbidden from doing certain things due to an earlier transgression/false accusation, etc.) so the player has to act as their body and/or mind. One of my students wrote a post-apocalyptic game-story where one of the NPCs is a scientist. I asked him why the playable character was supposed to solve all the problems when the scientist could easily do it herself. After being stymied, I reminded my student that he could "change the story to solve the problem" (a quote from the TV show *SuperWhy*). He then rewrote it so the player finds the scientist gasping for air on the side of the road. The loss of oxygen explained the loss of brain cells. This then allowed the scientist to remember just enough to provide some scaffolding but not enough to solve the problems herself. There are other approaches to solving the Dumbledore problem as well. For example, the helper could be like Hermoine—Harry's friend who is just as ignorant as he is to whatever hidden information there is but who has superb research skills and a clever mind. Or different NPCs can have different pieces of information that on their own don't mean anything but when put together by the main character indicate what actions need to be taken. Ghosts can make excellent helpers because they can provide information about the past. In that same vein, time travelers can bring information back from the future. In my coding class, there are two helpers who are friends of the playable character, both modeled after people in my own life. One of them, Frank, is good at providing answers but not so good at explaining them, and the other, Tory, is the one who explains instead of answering, thus earning the nickname "Tory the Teacher." Students can reach out to either Frank or Tory depending on their needs; however, both links lead to my e-mail address, so I end up being the ultimate helper by playing both characters. I highly recommend having a helper role in your game-story that you play so you can provide the scaffolding Vygotsky (1978) recommends to keep students in their challenge zones.

One problem with helpers that Dille and Platten (2007) point out, though, is that the player should be the hero. If the player is constantly being "bossed around" by being told what to do by helpers, that can make the player feel disempowered:

> When you have Nagging Nancy storytelling where every other character in the world is saying: "Go here… go there…see this guy…get this thing," the game has become a series of chores and the hero is now a messenger boy.
>
> (p. 17)

A solution to this is to have the player make active choices; in other words, instead of having others "say it," have the hero "play it" (Dille & Platten, 2007). You can have NPCs telling the hero opposite things (devil on one shoulder, angel on the other) so the hero is making an active choice; you can have the hero actively seek information by making a phone call, having to beat up or trick an NPC into giving up information, or even have to compliment an NPC first or establish trust by confiding something. You can even have the hero overhear a conversation, making them feel privy to secret information. Playing as an NPC in your game allows you to provide scaffolding, guidance, and direction without disrupting the flow of the gameplay.

Another option is to "display it" (Dille & Platten, 2007)—have billboards give hints and other signs in the environment to indicate what the player has to do. In my *Zombie School* game, there are signs in the campus center for the cafeteria, the arcade, and the career center. The signs give the player options without someone telling the player what to do, allowing the player to make an active choice. Going to the career center leads them to realize they want to teach in order to "prepare zombie kids to be successful in the zombie apocalypse" and sets them on the path to student teaching. At one point in the game, they need some rest and relaxation, but playing too many arcade games means not enough time spent on lesson planning. Never visit the cafeteria, and players aren't taking care of themselves and don't have enough energy to be a good student teacher. When deciding what to wear for the first day of school, players use a cell phone to explore the social media of different people in the school to see what they are wearing. Players have to imitate the right person on the right social media site to get it correct. There are lots of ways you can "display it" in your game instead of having endless dialogue trees.

While the helpers aid the playable character in making progress, the hinderers, on the other hand, block progress. They can be gatekeepers, tricksters, guards, enemies, or any other character who puts up challenges to the achievement of the protagonist's goal. In fact, in some cases, the environment itself can act like a hinderer character by putting up barriers and causing chaos. In many videogames, the enemies that players have to defeat at the end of a level in order to level up are called "level bosses." The major enemy at the end of the game is called "the big boss." While a lot of videogames feature a series of "bosses" the player has to overcome, remember that hinderers can sometimes turn into helpers, particularly if the hero is able to win them over, but helpers can also turn into hinderers or be hinderers, all along fooling the hero into thinking they are a helper. A dramatic element in your game-story might involve the player trying to figure out if an NPC is truly trying to help them or if that NPC is supplying disinformation to try to misdirect their actions. For example, readers of the Harry Potter series are constantly trying to guess if Snape is a helper or a hinderer. A key plot point in the *Myst* game-story revolves around which brother you trust. According to Dille and Platten (2007), "[Betrayals], especially when caused by player action, are more powerful than simple revelations" (p. 70). Using "conditional triggers," such as choosing an insult on the dialogue tree, can turn an ally into an enemy and vice versa. Having clear helpers and clear hinderers, and then throwing in a character who vacillates between the two can be a good game-story strategy.

There's also the helped. These types of NPCs show up most often in caretaking games where the player has to take care of an animal, someone who is hurt, a child, or maybe even an alien from another planet. For the Human Development class that I taught, I created a game where students have to take care of a baby with the player's various decisions impacting the child's growth. Anyone who took a class where they had to carry around a bag of flour or an egg as if it were a baby is familiar with this kind of simulation. Games with a character who is helped don't have to be serious life-or-death games. One of the students in my coding class created a game where the player helps an NPC pick out an appropriate outfit for different occasions.

In addition to helpers, hinderers, and the helped, sometimes game-stories have a special character who directs the action. This character type has different names—Fate, Dungeon Master, Drama Manager, Playwright—but, for our purposes, we are going to use the term Narrator. The narrator serves as the solution to what Ryan (2009) calls the "interactive paradox" (p. 45), the messiness of the player's choices, which may or may not lead to a coherent story, versus tight authorial control leading to a coherent story but with little user input. A narrator can balance on the tightrope between these two extremes by letting the gameplay play out until it needs redirecting or even a dramatic intervention because gameplay has gotten too boring. For example, one of my students had her students become different animals in an ecosystem. Each animal had their own Facebook page (posters on the walls of the classroom) where students had to draw their animal and write out their animal's profile, including likes and dislikes. They then had to friend each other; however, if prey friended a predator, they would be eaten, so they needed to know which friend requests to reject. Posting and responding to each other's statuses became a daily ritual. Once the class hit a lull, however, the teacher threw in a natural disaster, so the animals had to learn how to adapt in order to survive. The teacher is often the one who plays the narrator so they can control the action and be the impetus for learning.

PRACTICE GAME: Soul Searching For this practice game, I want you to think of a moral dilemma in your field. What is something people have grappled with in the past, present, or possibly will have to in the future? Now, think of who would be the decider of that moral dilemma—a Supreme Court Justice? The president? A scientist? An ordinary citizen who found themselves in that situation? For example, you might want to create a game like one of my students did where the player plays as a typical U.S. teenager in the early '70s whose draft number was pulled, and they have to decide whether or not to sneak off to Canada or fight in the Vietnam War. *Please note that software tools can change, so these instructions and visuals are as of the writing of this book.*

Directions: Use presentation software to create a *Choose Your Own Adventure*–type story where players make choices, which then lead to different follow-up slides with subsequent consequences.

Instructions: Open up Google Slides or PowerPoint or some other presentation software tool. On that first slide, put the title of the game and insert a picture about the dilemma. On the next slide, write out the backstory in second person and insert a picture of the playable character. On the next slide, present the moral dilemma and use Insert/Shapes to draw two (or more) boxes. In each box, add text that describes that choice. Then, create two (or more) slides describing the outcome of those decisions. Go back to the decision slide with the boxes, click on one of the boxes to highlight it, then go to Insert/Link and, in the popout, select "Slides in This Presentation" for Google Slides or "Place in This Document" for PowerPoint, then choose the slide that has the outcome of that decision choice. Do the same for the other choice. Now, for each outcome, create another dilemma and do the same linking to other slides with those choices, and so on. I know the mathematicians among us are saying, "Wait a minute. That is going to get exponentially large pretty quickly!" That is correct! However, there are ways to "prune" your branching tree. One is to have some choices lead back to the same outcome (Crawford (2013) calls this a "foldback" (p. 121)). Another is to have some choices lead to dead ends, often literal dead ends where the character dies (with, of course, the option to try again). Whatever you do, make sure each path has its own resolution.

Visual Aid:

FIGURE 3.1 PowerPoint Internal Linking Example.

Congratulations! You just created your first digital *Choose Your Own Adventure* game!

How Can Characters Interact with Each Other?

Having other characters allows for interactivity, which Crawford (2013) defines as "a cyclical process in which two agents alternately listen, think, and speak" (p. 28). I would expand the definition of interactivity to a cycle of observation, reflection, and reaction, or, even more expansively, receiving input, processing, and producing output, as interacting with others does not necessarily have to involve speech. For example, in the video game *Way* there are two characters who don't speak the same verbal language so they have to use body language to communicate. Since we have expanded our notion of characters to include non-human characters, both animals and objects, this extended definition of interactivity can serve us well.

Videogames have dealt with interactivity in different ways. Some video games, such as fighting games, are almost solely about physical interaction, although often some verbal insults are slung around as well. In these games, joysticks and buttons on the game controller map onto the actions of the player while the NPC opponent follows pre-defined response rules. With the advent of Wii and Kinect, gaming consoles can now "read" player's behavior as input. Google's free Teachable Machine (https://teachablemachine.withgoogle.com/) can be programmed to recognize different poses in addition to images and sounds, opening up possibilities for us amateur game designers. For example, you could use the Teachable Machine to create your own version of *Way* to help students learn how to read body language in order to communicate with each other.

Dille and Platten (2007) contend that game designers should use a "Play it, Display it, Say it" (p. 16) priority order, arguing that players should only say it if it can't be displayed or played.

However, there are plenty of videogames where language is key, especially those where human interaction drives the gameplay. Some use natural language processors similar to *ChatGPT* and other AI tools to simulate interactivity. The game *Façade* (2005), where you play as a dinner guest of a couple on the brink of separating, is one of the first examples of this. Others use parsers, which are software tools limited to recognizing only certain words to which it can then generate a response. *Eliza (1964)*, a program designed by Joseph Weizenbaum to imitate a therapist by responding to certain words and phrases (for example, talking about your mother), was a trailblazer in the area of parsers and even fooled some people into thinking they were interacting with an actual human being. For our purposes as teachers with limited resources, we will likely use either our actual students as "natural language processors" or dialogue trees. Many commercial games also use dialogue trees, even big box ones such as the *Legend of Zelda* series, where the player is given a list of possible quotes to say with the NPC's response dependent upon what the player chooses.[4] Dialogue trees are easy to create. In fact, I'm going to have you create one right now.

ACTION ITEM: Dialogue Tree You are going to use a survey tool to create a dialogue tree where players choose how to respond. *Please note that software tools can change, so these instructions and visuals are as of the writing of this book.*

Directions: Using a survey tool, create a multiple-choice item where the chosen response leads to different outcomes.

Instructions: Start a new Google Form. In the description type, "Will you marry me?" For the first item, choose a multiple-choice question format and type "Should you say yes or should you say no?" for the prompt. Then, for Option 1, type in "Yes." For the second multiple-choice answer option, type "No." These are the dialogue choices of the player. Then, in the menu that is on the right-hand side, click the equal sign twice to create two new sections.

Title the first one "Yes" and the second one "No." Use your imagination to type in what happens if the player says yes and what happens if the player says no. Now, go back to that original multiple-choice question where the player chooses how to respond and click on the three vertical dots in the lower right-hand corner. Choose "Go to section based on answer." You will see that next to each answer choice is now a drop-down menu. Click the down triangle and choose the relevant section—either Yes or No. After the second section, be sure to change the option below that section to "Submit Form"; otherwise, when that option is chosen, it will then go to the other response as well. Now, click on the Preview eye at the top right-hand corner and test it out.

Visual Aid:

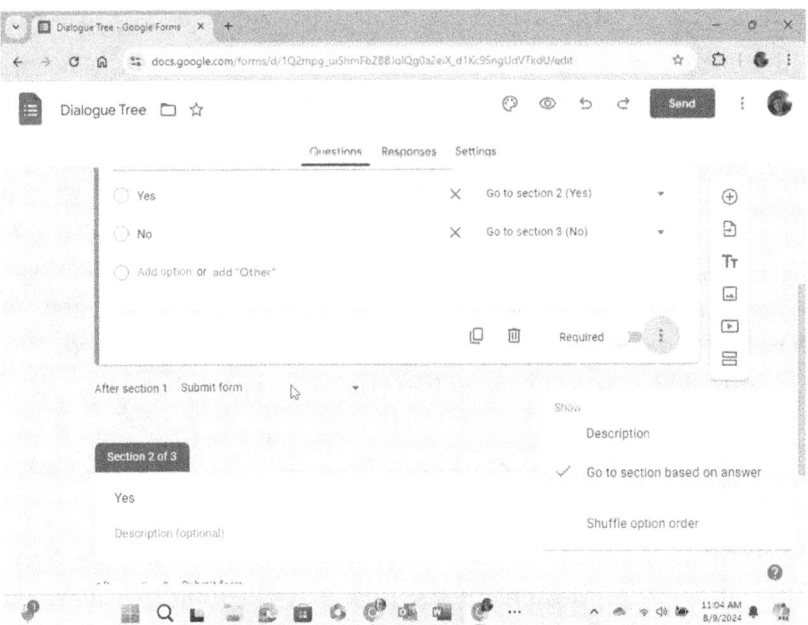

FIGURE 3.2 GoogleForm Branching Example.

You just created your first dialogue tree! Congratulations!

You likely made the connection that this is similar to what you did earlier in PowerPoint/Google Slides where you created your first *Choose Your Own Adventure* game, and you would be correct. All of these tools offer this internal linking capability that allows the designer to bypass linearity so the user can make choices.

Conclusion

Having the player be the "you" of the story gives students agency. This can be especially powerful for students who lack agency in their lives and for students who get to "be" a profession in which they have not seen people with their own backgrounds represented. Spreading out the backstory so that students discover bits and pieces so that they must do the mental work of putting it together to form a coherent story furthers this sense of ownership. Making decisions as the playable character and experiencing the consequences of those decisions leads to learning in context. All of this contributes to fostering students' "growth mindsets" (Dweck, 2007)—the notion that effort makes a difference, instead of the all too common sense among students that schooling is what is done to them. By embodying the playable character and immersing themselves in that character's story, students will likely learn curricular material willingly in order to achieve the playable character's goals. We will know that we have achieved our goal of having students lose themselves in the story when they use first-person when speaking about their playable character.

Chapter 3 Worksheet: Character Sheets

Directions: Fill out the following worksheet first for the playable character and then for the NPCs, replicating the chart for as many NPCs as you have. For each category, you can write "player's choice" or "N/A" if you decide it's better to leave it undefined. Plan to return to this to refine it as your game evolves.

Creating the Characters (Somebody)

Playable Character	Initial Ideas	Possible Alternatives
Name		
Occupation		
Skills		
Special ability or tool		
Appearance		
Dispositions		
Virtues		
Vices		
Values		
Goals		
Fears		
Backstory		
How does the character change over the course of the game? What prompts this change? How will you show this change?		

Non-playable Character	Initial Ideas	Possible Alternatives
Name		
Relation to main character (helper, hinderer, helped)		
Occupation		
Skills		
Special abilities		
Appearance		
Dispositions		
Virtues		
Vices		
Values		
Goals		
Fears		
Backstory		

Notes

1. When I asked my own kids what they call the character the player plays in a game, initially they said "me" and then, when I clarified my question, they both said "you."
2. In one of my first game-based courses, I had an NPC representing me as the teacher. When I had my sister playtest it, she said, "Why is Rachel in your game?," referring to the character of Rachel from *Friends* played by Jennifer Anniston, and I realized that I had, indeed, created my avatar to look how I would love to look.
3. According to Boller and Kapp (2017), "In learning games, cooperation is often a better element to use than competition, unless the competition is with the game itself. If you do opt for competition, consider a cooperative element as well, such as having teams of players" (p. 55).
4. My sister contends that her daughter learned to read so she could read the dialogue choices in a *Legend of Zelda* game.

References

Blanchard, J. (2007, December 29). Anti-bullying program aims to teach students empathy. *Seattle Post-Intelligencer*.

Crawford, C. (2013). *On interactive storytelling*. Berkeley, CA: New Riders.

Dille, F. & Platten, J. S. (2007). *The Ultimate guide to videogame writing and design*. New York, NY: Lone Eagle Publishing Company.

Dweck, C. (2007). *Mindset: The new psychology of success*. New York: Ballantine Books.

Erikson, E. (1950). *Childhood and society*. New York: W.W. Norton.

Jackson, J. (2007). *Unmasking identities: An exploration of the lives of gay and lesbian teachers*. Lanham, MD: Lexington Books.

Jenkins, H. (2009). *Confronting the challenges of a participatory culture: Media education for the 21st century*. Cambridge, MA: MIT Press.

Kellinger, J. (2017). *A guide to designing curricular games: How to "game" the system*. Cham, Switzerland: Springer.

Mateas, M. & Stern, A. (2006). Interaction and narrative from *Expressive AI*. In K. Salen and E. Zimmerman (Eds.), *The game designer reader: A rules of play anthology* (pp. 642–669) Cambridge, MA: MIT Press.

Prensky, M. (2002). The motivation of game play, or the REAL 21st century learning revolution. *On the Horizon, 10*(1), 5–11.

Rabin, S. (2009). *Introduction to Game Development* (2nd ed.). Herndon, VA: Cengage Learning.

Richter, J & Livingstone, D. (2011). Multi-user games and learning. In S. Tobias and J. D. Fletcher (Eds.), *Computer games and instruction*, (pp. 101–124). Charlotte, NC: Information Age Publishers.

Rusch, D. (2017). *Making deep games: Designing games with meaning and purpose*. Boca Raton, FL: CRC Press.

Ryan, M. (2009). From narrative games to playable stories: Toward a poetics of interactive narrative. *Storyworlds: A Journal of Narrative Studies, 1*, 43–59.

Saltsman, A. (2019). Plot generators. In T. Short & T. Adams (Eds.), *Procedural storytelling in game design*, (pp. 295–302). Boca Raton, FL: CRC Press.

Schell, J. (2008). *The art of game design: A book of lenses*. Burlington, MA: Morgan Kaufmann.

Sheldon, L. (2014). *Character development and storytelling for games* (2nd ed.). Course Technology PTR: Boston, MA.

Short, T. (2019). Maximizing the impact of generated personalities. In T. Short & T. Adams (Eds.), *Procedural storytelling in game design* (pp. 271–282). Boca Raton, FL: CRC Press.

Swan, R. (2010). Feedforward as an essential active principle of engagement in computer games. In R. Van Eck (Ed.), *Gaming and cognition: Theories and practice from the learning sciences* (pp. 108–136). Hershey, PA: Information Science Reference.

Sylvester, T. (2013). *Designing games: A guide to engineering experiences*. Sebastopol, CA: O'Reilly Media.

Travers, M. (2022). *Volcano vision*. Game created for EDC G 634 Introduction to Game-based Teaching taught by J. Kellinger at UMass Boston.

Vygotsky, L. (1978). *Mind in society*. Cambridge, MA: Harvard University Press.

Gee, J.P. (2003). *What videogames have to teach us about learning and literacy*. New York: Palgrave Macmillan.

Boller, S., & Kapp, K. (2017). *Play to learn: Everything you need to know about designing effective learning games*. Alexandria, VA: ATD Press.

4

Developing Goals (Wanted)

You are embarking on a journey through time with a mission to try to change the course of history. You are armed with knowledge and foresight. You know what mistakes have been made and you must use that knowledge and foresight **to change the events that ultimately led to the worst genocide in modern history**. *A lot of questions have been swirling in your head. How does something of this magnitude actually happen in a developed nation? How was the world just able to stand by and watch it happen? And, ultimately, do we have a responsibility to get involved in another country's affairs to prevent human rights crimes?*

(Sandra Schwarzkopf, *Foresight*, 2019)

Now that we have identified who the player is going to be, we need to identify what their goal is; otherwise, you have no story because what drives stories and engages the readers and viewers is our investment in whether or not the protagonist achieves their goal. Without a goal, you also have no game because games are essentially goal-driven play. In the previous excerpt from one of my student's games, this time-traveling character's goal is to "change the events that ultimately led to the worst genocide in modern history." Give careful thought to the character's goal and what message it sends. For example, I had a student who wanted to design a game where her students played leaders of different countries racing to get the atomic bomb so they could deploy it first. After discussing the implications of this, she changed it so that the race was to get the atomic bomb first to prevent other countries from getting it and using it, sending a message of peace instead of that of death and destruction.

You could design a game where the playable character's goal is to choose a goal—for example, if the character has two incompatible "wanteds." I just read a book, *The Rule of Four*, where the main character has to choose between solving the puzzles within an ancient book or being with his girlfriend because he finds that the book draws him in so completely that he loses all sense of time, meaning, and relationships. On the other hand, instead of having the player choose between two things they love, the game could consist of deciding which goal is the lesser of two evils. Setting up a game like this would certainly foster some interesting classroom discussions, whether you design it so the whole class has to decide together or so that individuals, partners, or small groups make their own decisions, which are then reflected upon during debriefing.

According to Epstein (2019), "A good story has a character we care about, with an opportunity, problem or goal, who faces obstacles and/or an antagonist and/or character flaws, who has something to lose (jeopardy), and something to gain (stakes)" (p. 230). Often, the "caring about the character" comes with identifying with their goal. If the main playable character has a goal students believe in and can identify with, they will find the game more compelling. This may mean making the character the same age as your students. There is a reason so many heroes in young adult books are adolescents. While unlikely in the real world, making it seem and feel possible for teenagers to be that character saving the world makes the story more engaging to that audience and fosters a sense of agency. You see what I did there? Iterative design. I referred back to the "Somebody" chapter, having you rethink and revise your character based on the character's goal. What is important to remember is that the character's goal should reflect what the character values and the lessons you want to convey. There is a reason this step in the story design process is called "Wanted."

While the playable character's goal should enable the unit goals to be achieved, they are not necessarily the same as the game's goals. Sometimes there are both overt and covert goals of a game, a "Trojan Horse" game (Chatham, 2011, p. 78) if you will. For example, Johnson (2012) claims that *World of Warcraft*, a massive multiplayer online role-playing game (MMORPG) where avatars fight monsters and each other, is really about natural selection, although few would describe it as such. Johnson (2012) also points out that *Super Mario Bros.* is really about timing, not plumbing. One of my students created a branching narrative game where students play the main character of *Mansfield Park*. When players made choices that departed from the novel, the consequences designed by my student mirrored what would have likely happened in that time period—for example, deciding not to get married as a woman during that time period had very different results than today. This game was not about trying to make the same decisions as the main character but rather about learning how that historical time period impacted people's choices. A classic example of having an ulterior motive is the mentor character in *Karate Kid* having the main character paint fences, wax a car, etc., which turned out to be the same physical movements he needed to use to defeat his enemy. In my previous book about game-based teaching, I framed it with a game-story where a teacher time travels to the future to design the ultimate teaching tool since all the teachers were deliberately targeted in World War III according to the game-story. At the beginning, the reader/player has to write up a proposal to convince the commander that games are the optimal teaching tool, with the stealth objective of getting my students to think about how they could defend game-based teaching if a parent or principal opposed it.

Analogies and metaphors are often a good way to achieve this duality because they create a "transfer bridge" between students' prior knowledge and new knowledge. This may explain why, according to Schell (2008), "every successful videogame finds a way to combine something familiar with something novel" (p. 279). For example, one of my research participants used a parking garage metaphor to describe atoms to his students. My own children and I are reading the *Divergent* series, and we have an ongoing debate about whether or not the divergent (characters in that story world who have abilities that match multiple factions) represent the oppression of queer people or that of people who are neurodivergent. An amusement park might make for a good game setting, with the Ferris Wheel representing something that repeats, the Hall of Mirrors something confusing, roller-coasters the ups and downs of life, carnival games to practice skills, and so forth. Looking for similarities is a great way to make connections. In my overly complicated game where students play as a detective who goes undercover as a new teacher, the main character realizes that being a detective is much like teaching—looking for patterns and making inferences from data to assess what students know and can do. While metaphors are a great way to employ "stealth learning" (MacCullum-Stewart, 2011), depending on the ages and sophistication of your students, you may need to have a debriefing session to explain the connection; otherwise, transfer might not happen.

What Are Some Common Game-story Archetypes?

Fortunately, there are a plethora of story archetypes you can choose from when determining the playable character's overarching goal. We have already discussed the Zombie Apocalypse idea and some various permutations you can use with zombies. Extrapolating from the Zombie Apocalypse is the overarching "Slaying the Monster(s)" type game. We can see this theme throughout time, starting with Beowulf defeating Grendel to the Arthurian legends about slaying dragons to Godzilla movies to any number of current books, movies, and TV shows, such as

Stranger Things. These enemy-defeating stories often come packaged in the larger hero archetype described by Joseph Campbell in *A Hero with a Thousand Faces* (1949/2008). The gist of the archetype is as follows:

1) The main character has a **call to adventure**, often to search for something (an enchanted ring, justice, retribution, equality, answers).
2) The main character initially **refuses** to answer the call.
3) The main character **decides to do it** anyway.
4) The main character **travels away** from their familiar world into an unfamiliar one.
5) The main character **has an older mentor** teach them the ways of this new world.
6) The main character **overcomes many obstacles**, including enemies, monsters, and temptation, sometimes by brute force, sometimes by trickery, sometimes by being strategic, sometimes by luck.
7) The main character **achieves the goal** of the call to adventure.
8) The main character **returns home a changed person**.

ACTION ITEM: Go to YouTube or any other video search engine. Type in "Bill Moyers interview Joseph Campbell *Star Wars*" and watch the video where Joseph Campbell discusses how *Star Wars* fits the hero archetype.

In my Introduction to Game-Based Teaching class, I have students find examples of the hero archetype. It always amazes me the wide variety of stories they identify that follow this template, such as *Moana, The Lego Movie, Pride and Prejudice, Shrek, Buffy the Vampire Slayer, Finding Nemo*, and so on with one student writing, "I could do this all day." Many videogames follow the hero archetype as well. Ryan (2009) has an explanation for this:

But how can a story be created when the user's possibilities of action are limited to moving, picking up objects, manipulating them, and solving riddles through this manipulation, as is the case in [many video] games? The most obvious way to handle this problem is to choose a type of plot that puts great emphasis on physical actions. This explains why the archetypal narrative pattern described by...Joseph Campbell (1968/1973) has been so popular in computer games: a hero receives a mission, fulfills it by performing various tasks, and gets rewarded in the end. The deeds of the hero are relatively easy to simulate through the game controls, the basic sequence of accomplishment-reward can be repeated endlessly, allowing the player to reach higher and higher levels in the games, the script lends itself to great variations in setting and in the nature of the tasks, and the solitary nature of the hero's quest makes interpersonal relations dispensable.

(p. 50)

The timeless, cross-genre, and multiple-media appeal of the hero archetype suggests that it has something compelling about it that draws all of us. I urge you to consider this basic framework for your game-story.

However, the hero archetype is not the only archetype out there. Mystery is one that can work well with lots of subject areas. This book already mentioned "mysteries of history," but if you think about it, science is all about solving "mysteries," and experts in every subject area seek answers to questions. Solving a mystery can make a great videogame; after all, as Rouse (2019) points out, "Mysteries are essentially stories as puzzles" (p. 161). Some common mysteries might involve solving a murder, figuring out who you are after waking up with amnesia, or tracking down a stolen painting. Tracking down a stolen painting can be a great way for world language students to practice the target language. I have had several world language teachers use this archetype in their curricular games. Some of the best ones have been analog games where every day the teacher sets up a different scenario—buying a ticket at the train station using the target language, finding out information from an informant at a café, which involves not only conversation but also ordering correctly off a menu—and arranging the classroom for these different settings. The teacher then has the students begin on one side of the room practicing for that day's challenge. When students are ready, they come up to the ticket window set up by the teacher to try to buy a train ticket to the correct destination or to a table and chairs to glean information from an informant while ordering off a menu in a makeshift café or whatever the scenario is. If they are not successful, they go back to the practice area. If they are successful, they "graduate" to the other side and become the NPCs themselves, determining if the students trying the challenge are successful or not; that way, multiple students can try the challenge at the same time. The stolen painting scenario, however, is not just for world language teachers. Art history (having to use your knowledge of different genres or historical periods to solve the mystery) or history (think Nazis stealing paintings), physical education (slipping into the thief's apartment to find clues or, even better, being the thief and having to evade the laser beams, i.e., strings, or avoid triggering a motion detector camera can involve plenty of physical skills), science (analyzing the type of paint and discovering a painting is fake), math (using geometry to figure out how the thief managed to get the painting out of the museum), or English (use those persuasive skills!) can all rely on the stolen painting, or stolen anything, story frame. Using your classroom as the gamespace by rearranging desks, decorating, or putting tape on the floor, such as a grid for a graph, creates intrigue and immersion. Imagine how engaged students would be if they walked into your room to find a taped outline of a body on the floor![1] Mysteries are essentially solving a problem, so thinking of problems that are common in your field can be a fruitful way of coming up with the character's goal.

Another common technique is time travel, like the game snippet at the beginning of this chapter or the game-story from my previous book on game-based teaching that I described earlier. Time travel can obviously be useful in history class and can allow students to engage in "counterfactual analysis," or posing and thinking through those "What if?" scenarios (e.g., what if the North had allowed the South to secede instead of having the U.S. Civil War? What if Al Gore had been declared the winner of the 2000 U.S. presidential election?). Some history teachers may balk at this, thinking that it is hard enough getting students to understand what actually happened and that asking them to pretend could lead some students to think that is what happened, but I contend that counterfactual analysis helps students *do* history by thinking through causes and effects instead of just reading about history, and a debriefing session can be used to uncover and debunk any misunderstandings. Time travel can be used in other subjects as well, such as English when examining utopias/dystopias or historical fiction, science with students doing experiments from the past, and using math to solve past problems or even future ones! The possibilities are endless.

Escape and/or survival stories lend themselves well to games. This can also cross subject areas. Physical education is an obvious one where students can use physical skills to run away or evade someone. Unfortunately, history provides too many escape and survival scenarios, particularly where enslavement and genocide are involved. Science can be used to figure out how to escape and survive (think *MacGyver*, the TV show where the main character uses science to repurpose everyday objects into the various tools he needs). Math calculations can also be used to escape. Remember, however, there does need to be a story. When my children were in middle school, I could not figure out why they weren't excited about the escape rooms they were doing in class until they described them. It turns out the "escape rooms" were really just digital worksheets where students had to solve random, unconnected math problems or answer questions in other subject areas to reveal "clues" in the form of letters that then formed a word, but there was no story behind this or even reason to do this except that it was assigned. A true escape room game has a game-story. For example, the "you" could be wrongfully imprisoned and have to use math to figure out the angle and timing to throw the fork that came with their food in order to stop the fan blades in the air conditioning vent so they can then use the chair to climb up into the vent to escape or whatever game-story the teacher makes up that requires math or another subject area to solve the challenges. Adding a ticking time bomb scenario can make an escape/survival game feel even more dire. It also doesn't even have to be the main character who needs to escape. It could be that the main character has to help someone escape. I created one game for a workshop presentation where a student was "trapped" in my online class and "interrupted" my video lecture. I used the excuse that I had to talk to IT to figure this out (thus removing me from the situation to solve the Dumbledore problem) and instructed my audience to use various features of a Learning Management System to try to free the student. Designing a survival game taps into some of our most basic instincts.

Creating a game using missing information or disinformation can also work really well. For example, the playable character could be faced with a situation where they have to disguise themselves and pretend to be someone else. Or perhaps someone is an impostor, but the playable character has to figure out who they really are. Or perhaps the playable character suspects that some information is disinformation and they have to figure out which information is wrong and which is correct. That can work in any subject area!

> **ACTION ITEM:** Next time you have a lot of information that you have to convey to your students, make one of the pieces of information wrong in a way that students can figure out it is wrong. Then, before you begin the lesson, tell the students you are going to say one thing that is wrong and that you will award extra credit to the first person who figures it out. Gauge students' attention levels. If you are a teacher who teaches the same class multiple times a day, do it with one class but not another and compare the differences in students' attention and retention.

One of my students created a game where the playable character finds a burnt spell book on their way home from school. They then have to use morphemic analysis to figure out the missing words so they can perform different spells to ward off various enemies and solve different problems. Remember, information is a valuable resource, particularly when it is private. After all, the game of *Clue*, where each player gets a set of private information and selectively shares data with other players, is all about information as a resource. Filling in missing information, identifying mis and/or disinformation, and figuring out what information is irrelevant are all useful story ideas that can be used in any subject area.

If none of these work for you and you cannot think of another story idea, you can always use getting a job in that field. This comes with passing an interview, going through orientation, learning on the job, making mistakes on the job, and learning from these mistakes. While this may sound boring at first, there are ways to spice this up. The "getting and performing a job" story frame is what I did for my Designing Curriculum and Instruction class where students play as new teachers. Students have to pass an interview (the secret is that they have to use keywords from the school's mission statement) and then go through orientation. During the preplanning period, students attend professional development in the mornings and, in the afternoons, plan their curriculum with the help of someone who is new to that school but was a teacher for a few years elsewhere. This dual track of morning activities and afternoon activities helped solve my problem of students having to wait for me to grade something before being able to move on because they could work on one track while waiting for me to grade something on the other one. At one point, the veteran teachers take the newbie—i.e., the playable character—out for drinks. While at the bar, the veteran teachers challenge the player to a drinking game where the player has to identify which curricular ideology each veteran teacher belongs to. Having the veteran teachers belong to different curricular ideologies allowed me to orchestrate conversations among them where distinctions, overlaps, and nuances among these curricular ideologies are explored without me biasing my students with my own beliefs, like I probably did when I taught this class as a traditional class. When school starts in the game-story, the player has to navigate the first few days of school. Then the principal calls for an emergency faculty meeting because one of the veteran teachers has been accused of helping his students cheat on the state's standardized test. The newbie player has to save the day by relying on what they learned about data analysis in professional development to explain the anomalies in the students' test scores. Now that I think of it, being a first-year teacher is a game of survival! There are reasons you went into the field you did, whether you are a career changer or a lifelong teacher of that subject matter. Tap into what interested you about that field to craft a story with compelling challenges of being new on the job.

PRACTICE GAME: Heroic Adventure This time, I am going to have you explore a tool you may not be familiar with, *Twine*, a free narrative branching tool at https://twinery.org. Don't worry, I'll be gentle. This is really what you have been doing all along, where players make choices, just in another tool and with some added features. I want you to first try figuring out what to do based on the directions. If you need more help, you can follow the instructions. If you need to, you can view the visual aid or just use the visual aid to check your work. *Please note that software tools can change, so these instructions and visuals are as of the writing of this book.*

Directions for Call to Adventure Story Segment: You are going to create the first story segment, a Call to Adventure, in which you describe someone coming to ask "you" to go on an adventure. In doing so, that person will refer to you by name. At that point, you will have the player input it as a variable. You will then have the main character decide whether to stay or go by creating links to two new story segments.

Instructions for Call to Adventure Story Segment: After going to Twine at https://twinery.org, click on New and name your story. Double-click in the box for the first story segment. Click "Rename" to name the passage (you can name it "Call to Adventure"). In the box, write about a "call to adventure." Keep it simple for now; this is just practice. Remember when you write your story to use "you" for the main character. When you have an NPC, ask the main character to go on an adventure, have the player input their name by Clicking Macro, choosing Input, adjusting the input box size, typing "Input your name" in the first field, check "Bind this element to the variable," and then write "name" in that variable field. End the passage with "Should you stay or should you go?" Then go to Macro, Link and put the text you want to show up (it could just be "stay") and the name of the new passage (also could be "Stay"). Then, do the same for going. You can move the boxes around on the grid to where they make sense to you.

Visual Aid for Call to Adventure Story Segment:

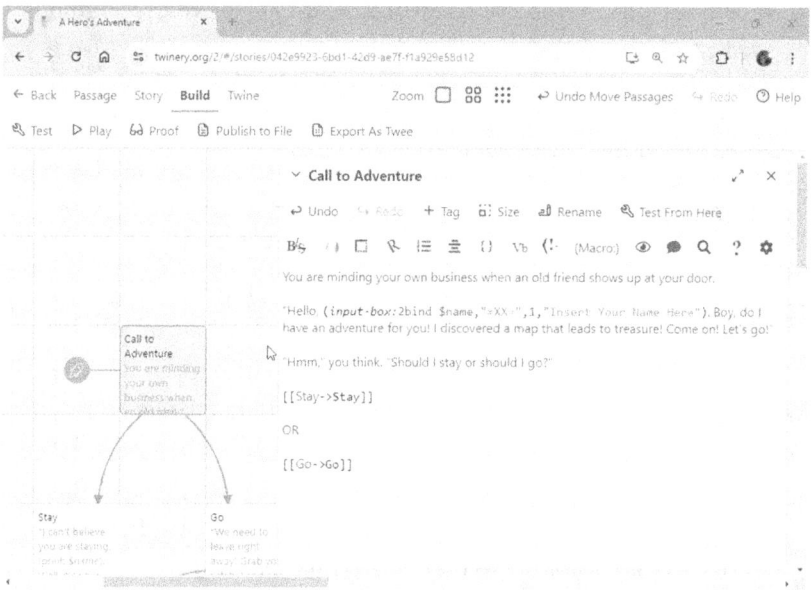

FIGURE 4.1 Twine Branching Example.

Directions for the Stay and Go story segments: Write out what happens if the player chooses to stay. Include in that someone saying their name by using the variable where you stored their name. For the Go story segment, have the player choose an item to bring with them and save that item in a variable.

Instructions for the Stay and Go story segments: In the "Stay" box, write out what happens if the player chooses to stay. In that box, have someone call the main character by their name by typing this: (*print*: $name) in the text. You can have that be a dead end if you want, or you can give them the option to change their mind. In the "Go" box, have the player choose one item to bring by clicking Macro, clicking Input, choosing Dropdown menu, and typing in the options. Click Bind to variable and name the variable "item." Click "Test from here." When you test it, you will notice only the first option shows up until you scroll down through the dropdown menu because the menu background is white and the text is white. To fix that, right before the dropdown menu, change the text color to another color by typing (text color: red) or whatever color you choose.

Visual Aid for Stay and Go Story Segments:

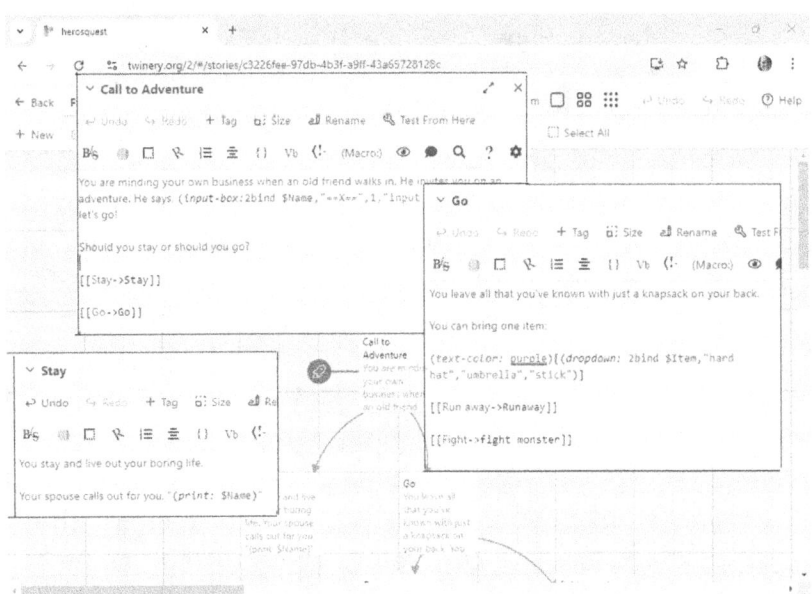

FIGURE 4.2 Twine Branching Example with Dropdown Menu.

Directions for Monster encounter: At the end of the Go story segment, have a monster confront the player and have the player decide whether to fight or run away by creating links to those two story segments. Write out what happens if the player runs away. If the player fights, have them win only if they choose a certain item. If they lose, have them suffer an amount of damage chosen at random from 1–6, and calculate the health as 20 – that amount of damage. Inform the player of how much damage and health they have.

Instructions for Monster encounter: At the end of the Go box, have the player encounter a monster. Create links to a "Run away" story passage and a stay and "fight" story passage. In the "Run away" box, write out what happens. You can have that as a dead end or a choice to go back and fight. In the stay and "fight" story passage, have the player take out the item chosen from the dropdown menu (*print*: $item). Then, go to Macro, If, scroll down to choose Variable, type in item, keep it as "is," and then type in one of the items. Click Add. In the box, you will see that after the If statement, it says, "Your text here." Type in "You defeated the monster!" or whatever text you want. Then, create another If statement, except use the dropdown menu to select "is not." Type in the same item as before. This time, type over the space that says, "Your text here" with something like "You lose!" or whatever text you want. Then, type "You have suffered" go to Macro, choose Value, type damage in the first field, choose random number and put in 1 and 6 for the between numbers. Click Add. Then type "(*print*: $damage) damage to your health. Your health is." Then, choose Macro, Value, type in health as the name of the variable, choose "coded expression," and type in 20-$damage for the code. Click Add. In the text box, type (*print*: $health).

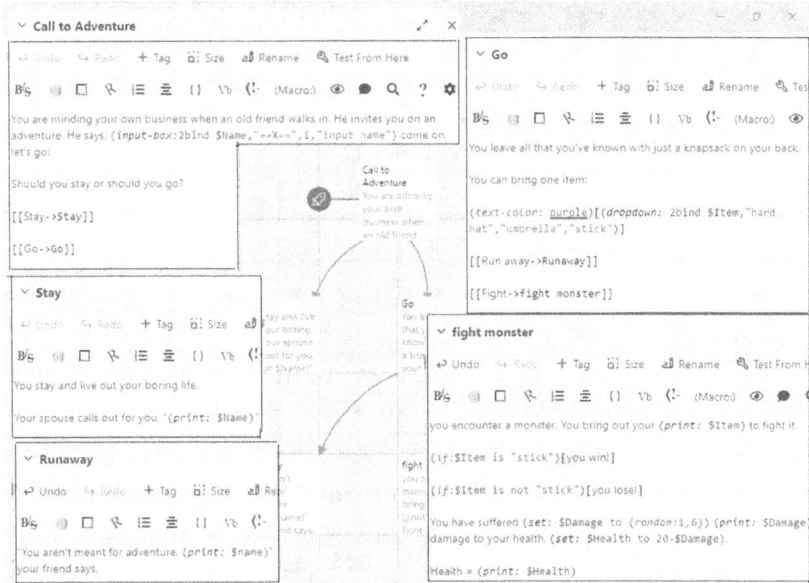

FIGURE 4.3 Twine Branching Example with Conditional Logic

Test it all out by clicking on the Call to Adventure passage box and selecting "Test from here." You just created your own text adventure game!!! Now, play around and experiment with it even more!

What Are Some Ways to Introduce the Goal to the Player?

As teachers, we are often advised to begin our lessons with a "hook." While not easy to do every single day, these hooks can really work wonders on student engagement. For example, I interviewed a science teacher who introduced her biology course by holding up a lit candle, referring to it as "Harvey," and insisting that Harvey is alive and challenging the students to counter that:

> Don't tell me any different! I know that Harvey is alive. See he moves. He excretes waste in the form of smoke.

He reproduces (as she holds a match to the flame, which then ignites). He needs oxygen to survive (as she starts to extinguish the flame by denying it oxygen). He can even die.

Students know that a flame is not a living being, so these statements create "cognitive dissonance" (Festinger, 1957), a term used to describe holding two contradictory beliefs—something humans are averse to doing and so are motivated to resolve which, in this case, they do so by trying to figure out what characteristics constitute living. Beginning a game with a contradiction, such as meeting a character who appears rich but has hints of being poor or, like in the videogame *Undertale* (spoiler alert), the encounter with Flowey the flower where he pretends to be nice but suddenly turns evil or any other number of appearances with a hint of being deceiving immediately arouses interest.

While creating cognitive dissonance can really hook a player, so can withholding information. Having an NPC say something like, "I dream of a day when we will be able to live above ground,"[2] introduces the goal while creating all sorts of suspense: What happened to force us to live underground? What is preventing us from going above ground? What can I do to enable us to live above ground? Having the player then find something that immediately gives a hint to some of these answers generates an early success, something videogame designers stress is important to hook players and make them feel successful, which will carry them through times when they struggle.

Conclusion

The main character's goal is what drives the story, so play out how different goals could lead to different outcomes and choose the one that you think can work best. Remember that, for our purposes, we need to choose a game goal where overcoming the obstacles to achieving that goal involves performing the core game mechanic, the "so" skill that completes the "Students will be able to" (SWBAT) statement. Once you think of the "Wanted," "promotype" (Hirumi and Stapleton, 2008, p. 134) your idea by running a one-liner description by your students, for example, a pirate trying to find hidden gold or a prisoner trying to escape or a coder trying to save the world from their own invention, to see how they react, ask your students if they think having a character pursue that goal would make an interesting game-story. You never know, your students might even tweak it or have an idea of their own that you can run with!

Chapter 4 Worksheet: Revisiting the Design Document

Directions: Go back to your design document from chapter two. Fill out the second column (or copy and paste) with what you had for Chapter 2. Considering what you have learned from reading this book so far and from running your ideas by your students, write down any changes, additions, or cuts you want to make to your ideas. While other categories may be loosely defined, at this point, the "So" skill should be fixed, and the main character's goal needs to be fleshed out.

	Ideas from Chapter 2	Changes, Additions, Cuts
Working Title		
Topic		
Target Audience (Grade level, class title, background info on students, player types if known)		
Core Game Mechanic (the "So" or SWBAT skill)		
Main Character/Player Avatar		

	Ideas from Chapter 2	Changes, Additions, Cuts
Backstory		
Main Character's Goal		
Obstacles		
Game-Story Structure (D&D, *Choose Your Own Adventure*, linear series of "well-ordered problems," emergent, etc.)		
Game Summary		
Feedback (Ask former and current students if they've ever played a game that touches on this topic; ask them how they would design a game about the topic; run your ideas by to get their input)		

Notes

1. Use with discretion, of course. If the community or a student had been subject to tragedy, this would not be appropriate and could have a triggering effect. This is one of the many reasons why it is imperative to know your students.

2. When my sister read this, she came up with this game-story beginning: "It's 2075 and you were born underground and have never seen the surface of the Earth. Above ground it is too hot and there are ravaging storms. It didn't used to be that way, there are stories shared about how life used to be, but the elders rarely talk about why things changed. You suspect it is because they feel guilty because they blame themselves." The game would then continue with the player traveling back in time to try to prevent the climate crisis.

References

Campbell, J. (1949/2008). *A hero with a thousand faces*. Novato, CA: New World Library.

Campbell, J. (1968/1973). *A hero with a thousand faces*. Princeton: Princeton UP.

Chatham, R. E. (2011). After the revolution. In S. Tobias & J. D. Fletcher (Eds.), *Computer games and instruction* (pp. 73–99). Charlotte, NC: Information Age Publishers.

Epstein, A. (2019). Dirty procedural storytelling in *We Happy Few*. In Tanya Short & Tarn Adams (Eds.), *Procedural storytelling in game design* (pp. 227–240). Boca Raton, FL: CRC Press.

Festinger, L. (1957). *A theory of cognitive dissonance*. Stanford, CA: Stanford University Press.

Hirumi, A. & Stapleton, C. (2008). Applying pedagogy during game development to enhance game-based learning. In C. T. Miller (Ed.), *Games: Purpose and potential in education* (pp. 127–162). New York: Springer.

Johnson, S. (2012). Theme is not meaning: Who decides what a game is about? In C. Steinkuehler, K. Squire, & S. Barab, (Eds.), *Games, learning, and society: Learning and meaning in the digital age* (pp. 32–39). New York: Cambridge University Press.

MacCullum-Stewart, E. (2011). Stealth learning in online games. In S. de Freitas & P. Maharg (Eds.), *Digital games and learning* (pp. 107–128). London: Continuum.

Rouse, R. (2019). Heavily authored dynamic storytelling in *The Church of Darkness*. In T. Short & T. Adams (Eds.), *Procedural storytelling in game design* (pp. 159–176). Boca Raton, FL: CRC Press.

Ryan, M. (2009). From narrative games to playable stories: Toward a poetics of interactive narrative. *Storyworlds: A Journal of Narrative Studies*, *1*, 43–59.

Schell, J. (2008). *The art of game design: A book of lenses*. Burlington, MA: Morgan Kaufmann.

Schwarzkopf, S. (2019). Foresight. In J. Kellinger (Eds.), *Game created for EDC G 634 introduction to game-based teaching taught*. Boston, MA: UMass Boston.

5

Designing the Game Obstacles (But)

*One day, while you are walking home from school alone, you notice something strange under a pile of leaves…the object turns out to be an ancient Book of Spells!… You open the book because you are a very curious person.… The problem with the Book of Spells is that, **since some of the pages are burned**, you will have to figure out what the spells say. Only correct spells can be used. If there are mistakes with your spells, you will transform into a mythical creature and will be trapped in the evil Mirkwood for 1,000 years.*

(Kristin Miller, *Radagast the Brown and The Noble Quest to Save Mirkwood*, 2019)

Jane McGonigal (2011) explains why games need obstacles, the "Buts," by using the game of golf. The goal of golf is to get a ball into several holes. If that was all there was to the game, then it would be a pretty boring game since all you would have to do is walk up to each hole and put the ball into it. It is the obstacle of having to hit the ball with a golf club from far away that creates the game. Same with stories. If Romeo and Juliet met at a dance, fell in love, and got married, it would not be the timeless story it is today. In the earlier game introduction, if this student of mine had just had players read out spells they found in a book, that would have been a pretty boring game and certainly not a learning one, that is, unless they are learning to read. When my own children were learning to read, we put labels on various items in the house. Our kids got bored pretty quickly, so we introduced a "but," an obstacle, by mislabeling items and playing "mix-upitis" (a name taken from one of their favorite TV shows at the time, *Doc McStuffins*) where they had to run around and put the labels back where they belonged. All stories, games, and game-stories need to have a good but.

What Are Some Different Types of "Buts"?

We all probably remember learning about conflict in high school English class with the categories of man versus man, man versus nature, man versus self. We can expand these beyond one gender to a person or, perhaps, even to a sentient being in order to be inclusive of different genders and nonhuman playable characters. We can also expand the types of conflict to fighting against machines (get ready for the AI robot revolution!), fighting against time (particularly good in puzzle games), fighting back against injustice (after all, what is *Angry Birds* but getting vengeance against those pigs who stole their eggs!), trying to change the past (with some time-traveling counter-factual analysis like in *Foresight*, the student game excerpt at the beginning of the previous chapter), trying to change the future (sentient being versus fate), fighting against the system (in the '60s, that would have been called fighting against "the man"), and there are probably even more types of conflict you, or your students, can think of. What you don't want, however, is "man versus random number generator" (Bartle, 1996/2006, p. 765). Regardless of how limiting or limitless your English teacher presented different types of conflict, the core essence of stories having to have conflict remains.

For your game-story, think about what types of conflict the playable character would need to encounter in order to use the core game mechanic—the "so"—to overcome them. What are the obstacles that could get in the way of the playable character achieving their goal? Are there natural disasters (for example, my student who had a natural disaster strike her ecosystem in her game)? Misinformation (the game with the geology glasses actually ended up being about having to counter misinformation to convince various townspeople about the impending doom)? Missing information (like in the burnt spell book at the beginning of this chapter)? Misplaced information (such as putting Odysseus' adventures in order as a result of someone dropping the manuscript and all the pages falling in random order)? Monsters (or a Zombie Apocalypse!)? Machines? People? Animals? Fate? Coincidences? Dumb luck?

Sometimes these "buts" take place as a series of obstacles. I am watching a television show where the main character has an overall goal (getting back to the United States), and every time she thinks she is getting closer, another obstacle is thrown into her face. To me, the *Legend of Zelda* game *Skyward Sword* felt like every time an obstacle was overcome, another one took its place![1] Beware, though, that students will equate "send[ing] the character out on meaningless, empty quests to fill time" (Rabin, 2009, p. 144) with busy work. For our learning games, it is important that these obstacles build on one another, just like we design our curricular units. Sometimes this involves going from small to large; for example, in my English Methods class, students start off tutoring, then lead small groups, and, lastly, teach the whole class. When practicing teaching each other at the end of the semester, I have the rest of the students role-play high school students and designate one to perform a "zinger"—a surprise such as pretending to throw up in class or a student coming out as gay—that the student teaching has to deal with. By doing this in a safe environment, the class can then debrief and students will feel better prepared when faced with real "zingers" when teaching for real. Sometimes having challenges increase in difficulty entails increasing in complexity, like in my coding class where students learn repeat loops before conditional loops. I knew I had created a series of "well-ordered problems" (Gee, 2007, p. 35) when a student said about my class, "You took us on a journey and each step felt logical and sequential." This "logical and sequential" can entail progressively removing scaffolding, cumulatively adding subtasks, and/or each challenge moving along the new Bloom's Taxonomy: remembering, understanding, applying, analyzing, evaluating, and creating (Anderson & Krathwohl, 2001, p. 67–68). However you organized the curriculum unit for your chosen topic is likely to fall in a "well-ordered" progression. Now, arrange the obstacles accordingly. According to Schell (2008), "It is an old maxim of Hollywood screenwriting that the main ingredients for a story are (1) A character with a goal and (2) obstacles that keep [them] from reaching [their] goal" (p. 270). Think of the Wanted as the long-term goal and the Buts as the short-term obstacles to overcome on the way to achieving the long-term goal.

One way to create a "but" is to limit the range of ways the playable character can attain their goal. Swan (2010) makes the point that going to a grocery store is a goal, whereas doing so on a tight budget or after finding out that you have diabetes is a challenge. Another option is to make resources hard to find. In one of the original videogames, *Adventure*, a bat picks up items (keys, treasures, etc.) and drops them in random places. The creator of that game describes this as "disturb[ing] the predictability of the game" calling the bat "the game's confusion factor" (Robinett, 1984/2006, p. 702). However you construct your obstacles, make sure you do so in a way that the core game mechanic, the skill that your students are mastering, is a tool to solving the obstacle, not the obstacle itself. For example, having to answer a monster's questions about fractions messages that fractions are an obstacle, but using fractions to figure out the ratios of ingredients to create a sleeping potion to get past the monster has students engage with fractions as a problem-solving tool. Creating obstacles that are in the context of blocking the playable character's ability to achieve their goal and doing so in a way that requires using the "so" skill embeds learning that skill into the game-story.

It helps here to think about skill versus chance. If your game is all chance, it feels random, uncontrollable, and very little to no learning (unless that's the lesson you want to impart—that life is random and meaningless). It might be easy to think then, particularly for a learning game, that everything should be skill-based. However, if it is all skill, a game can also lose its appeal because then it feels like chores. I find that mostly skill-based games with some surprises thrown in here and there tend to be the best balance. The big "but" or obstacle to achieving the goal is the first surprise, but some little surprises along the way can help bring levity and keep students on their toes. In one of my game-based courses, I included some Easter eggs, which are hidden objects, and I remember one of my students being so excited to find one she told me later that she rushed to tell her boyfriend. Some bigger surprises, though, can also add to the enjoyment of the game-story. In my designing curriculum class, one day there is a note on the door stating that there is an emergency faculty meeting where it turns out one of the veteran teachers has been accused of helping his students cheat on a standardized test. The student players then have to figure out what really happened. As long as the surprise doesn't feel completely out of the blue, surprises are great ways to create new obstacles while injecting some fun and some challenge into your game-story. After all, who doesn't like a plot twist or two?

What Are Some Different Ways You Can Embed Obstacles into Your Game?

At this point, you have a main character (Somebody) with some NPCs, a goal (Wanted), and some obstacles (Buts) to achieving that goal. You also started off with a "So"—your core game mechanic, i.e., skill you want students to improve upon. Now it is time to start creating a workable game. To do so, you need to take into consideration your constraints and affordances. Boller and Kapp (2017) boil these down to time, technology, people, and location (p. 40). *Time* involves how much time you have to create the game, which will determine what technology you use—none, something familiar, or learning something new—and how much class time you can devote to a curricular game (I would argue all the class time in the world! But I know there are lots of constraints to this, including the endless standardized testing that eats up so much class time). Not only is *technology* mediated by your own technological skills but also by what you can afford and have access to as well as the *people*, i.e., the students', learning curves. For example, a game for preschool kids needs to be much more intuitive and picture-based than for high school students. There are also cultural considerations. According to Dille and Platten (2007), "Americans are squeamish about sex in games. Japanese don't like to die too often. In Germany, there are huge issues about blood. It has to either not be there or be some funky color" (p. 61). The consideration of *people* can also include people beyond the students if you want to involve others in your gameplay. I had one ambitious student in my game design class who designed a game where other teachers in her school played different NPCs that her students could interview and another who had various teachers play villains that students had to locate and defeat. *Location*, including what technologies are available, is also a mediating factor. For example, do all students have access to a computer? Is there a computer lab? Do you want to create an analog game that takes place in your room? Outside? In the whole school? I had another student who put up QR codes in different locations around her school for her students to use their phones to gather information. From these descriptions and others in this book, you have probably gathered that you can use no technology (see the stolen painting description in Chapter 4), a combination (QR codes!), or full-on technology like in my asynchronous online coding class.

While it may feel intimidating, I do encourage you to "level up" your technology skills if you have the time. You already learned how to use internal linking in presentation software such as PowerPoint and Google Slides, in a survey tool like Google Forms, and in the branched narrative tool Twine. These lessons will take you a long way in your game-based teaching journey because they allow you to insert obstacles into the game-story— click here to save your dog from your burning house or click here to save the ancient heirloom that holds secrets of the past, or whatever "series of interesting decisions" (Meier, quoted by Prensky, 2011, p. 272) you introduce to your students. I have found PowerPoint quite powerful in terms of creating games, particularly *Choose Your Own Adventure*-type games. Not only can you create links to other slides by highlighting text, but you can also use action buttons—go to Insert/Shapes, scroll down, and choose an action button—for added functionality. The advantage of action buttons is that they allow you to assign sounds to them, end a slideshow (great at creating dead ends so your branching narrative does not get exponentially too big), put them in strategic places to create Easter eggs, and place them over a whole slide and make them transparent so the user does not even realize they are there. One of my students created a game where players had to click on various parts of a slide to explore a coral reef while avoiding the shark in the distance. By making action buttons transparent and placing them strategically, clicking on the sea anemone leads to a slide with a clownfish darting in and out of the sea anemone, whereas clicking on the darkness in the distance reveals the lurking shark. You can also create links to objects themselves, such as in my Romeo and Juliet game, where clicking on Romeo's pants on the floor shows a closeup of the necklace in his pocket that says Rosaline on the locket. Internal linking in presentation tools like PowerPoint makes them powerful game design engines.

In addition to the internal linking, PowerPoint allows you to copy and paste objects and erase their backgrounds, create custom motion paths for those objects to move around, and identify triggers that set off that motion or to show or hide objects. For example, one of my students created a game where the player has to successfully identify different types of igneous rock. When identified correctly, a checkmark appeared on top of the rock by using triggers (choose the object you want to appear, in this case the checkmark, go to animation and choose how you want it to appear, and then select the trigger, in this case the object that has to be clicked for the checkmark to appear). In this game, the player is a volcanologist (complete with the *Indiana Jones* theme playing in the background![2]), who is supposed to be monitoring a volcano. This student has a small action button of the map of the island on every slide that can be clicked at any time to go to the full map slide. I could not figure out how my student was able to design it so clicking on the full map slide led back to whichever slide the player just left since the action button (he overlayed a transparent action button over the entire map slide) options were previous slide, next slide, or a certain specific slide until I reverse engineered it and saw that he had chosen an option I had never noticed before—"last slide viewed." Always keep yourself open to learning from your students! This student also introduced his own surprise obstacle by having the player get bored, turn the seismograph into a radio, and use motion paths to show the player's avatar jumping off a cliff, landing in the water with a splash (using "after previous animation" for the splash to appear and then expand), swimming to the shore, and laying out to get a tan. As you can guess, the avatar then missed the warning signs that the volcano was about to erupt. This student has lots of "buts" in his game that get in the way of the playable character achieving their goal of monitoring the volcano to keep people safe.

> **ACTION ITEM:** Open up PowerPoint or any other software tool you commonly use and explore all the menu items. Try ones that you have no idea what they do to see what happens.

Transitions in PowerPoint are quite sophisticated. In fact, I just created some cutscenes for my coding class that I created in PowerPoint and then saved as videos just so I could use some of these transitions, such as the ripple effect to indicate a flashback and the fracture transition to show the avatar's vision breaking up when hit in the head. I created a Harry Potter game where one transition created the illusion of a piece of paper turning into an origami bird that flies off. The page-turning transition makes it easy to look like someone is flipping through the pages of a book. There is one transition that splits the screen in half in a way that looks like a door is opening, another that opens blinds, ones that you can use to indicate going into a dream state, and so forth. I also use PowerPoint as a graphic design studio—creating different items using its editing tools and saving a slide as a .png (which supports transparent backgrounds) or a .jpeg file. You can even save slides as animated GIFs![3]

Not all games created from presentation software have to be *Choose Your Own Adventure*–type games. I created a *Chemistry Escape* game where players have to figure out how to get to a key that is frozen inside a block of ice in order to unlock the door. In this game, I used triggered animations where players have to click on the correct Bunsen burner (which is the animation trigger), which then boils the liquid above it (assigning motion paths to white ovals and indicating that the animation should be repeated) and then click on the vial, which then triggers the vial to move along a motion path to pour liquid over the ice which, if the vial with the water is chosen after the Bunsen burner is clicked, will melt the ice to free the key. Clicking on the wrong vials leads to explosions or nothing at all happening, depending on the vial. One of the advantages of presentation software over some other tools you can use is that you can do a lot with visuals and animation.

If your game designed in a presentation tool becomes too complicated, then break it up into multiple presentations so that the player has to get to a certain place in order to be able to link

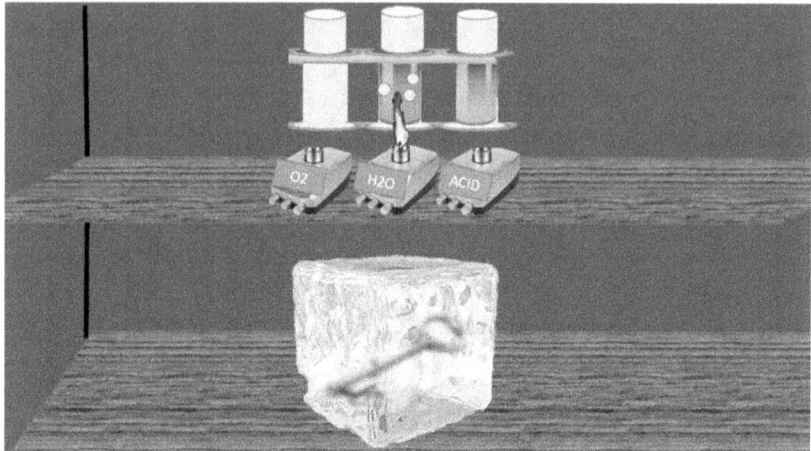

FIGURE 5.1 PowerPoint Slide from Chemistry Escape Game.

to the next presentation. I recommend having those breaks be between levels. You can even require a password (another obstacle!) that the player has to figure out through the gameplay in order to unlock the next level by encrypting the presentation with a password. One of my students did this very effectively with a math game where players had to be able to interpret coordinates (and solve equations to get the coordinates) of objects and then use a coordinate grid to locate those hidden objects in the classroom pictured on a slide. These objects, such as a cassette tape or a flash drive, held clues to the passwords. This was all part of a larger story that explained why everything had to be so secretive. Do not forget too that you can always copy a slide and/or a presentation and then make changes to keep some uniformity and cut down on excess work.

Do not limit yourself to one software tool. You can often blend tools without making it look too choppy. For example, for the Romeo and Juliet game I created, the player starts in Google Slides, but to unlock the locks on the dresser and nightstand (the obstacles), when players click on them, they lead to a Google

Form with the same picture of the lock that is in the slideshow. By selecting "Make it a quiz" in the settings, I use that Google Form so that students can only get to the link to the next Google Slideshow through the confirmation message if they get the answer correct. Using multiple Google Slideshows allowed me to copy the first slideshow and then insert a picture of the lock unlocked as the first slide, giving the player visual feedback that their answer worked. Depending on which lock is unlocked, a different slideshow is linked to that then requires players to unlock the second lock where, if done successfully, both lead to the final slideshow. In the final slideshow, which I created by copying the first slideshow, I added a lark and nightingale, which both fly to the balcony when the curtains are opened. This way I did not have to worry that this would accidentally happen when the curtains are opened in the first slideshow because the birds aren't even present in that one. I then saved all of these Google Slideshows in presentation mode only by erasing edit and everything after it in the URL and replacing it with preview?rm=minimal so that players couldn't cheat by using edit mode to look ahead (you can do the same with PowerPoint by saving it as a PowerPoint Show (.pps or .ppsx). By thinking creatively about how you can use different tools and how you can blend them together, you as the game designer can overcome a lot of obstacles through workarounds!

PRACTICE GAME: A Newbie Adventure in Three Acts For this practice game, we are going to use Google Forms. For the first section, describe your playable character, remembering to use "You," deciding to pursue a job in your subject area about a particular topic. Then, they hit their first "But"—they have to get hired. For the first three items, describe an interviewer asking them three (or however many you want) multiple-choice questions to see if they understand basic terms having to do with that topic. If they get any one of them wrong, they don't get the job and have to start over again. If they get them all correct, then they get hired. (Remember, click on the three vertical dots and select "Go to section based on answer" to be able to select which section to go to. To do this, you'll need to create the sections first.)

Players who are hired have to go to orientation (which can be a separate Google Form that they only get the link to if they get hired), where they learn how to do something. Using the File Upload option, require students to videotape themselves performing that task successfully in order to exit orientation (you can also have a multiple-choice or essay question they can only get right if they know how to perform that skill successfully if that works better). After the teacher has reviewed and approved this, students then get a link to the last Google Form.

In this last Google Form, a crisis has happened where players will have to use this skill to save people, the world, a treasure, themselves, or whatever makes sense. This is the big BUT of the story. For this last Google Form, the player has to apply this newly learned skill to different scenarios. For example, if they learned CPR, they would have to assess which NPCs need CPR and which don't.

What these three "acts" in Google Forms do is teach and assess declarative knowledge (knowing what something is), procedural knowledge (knowing how to do something), and conditional knowledge (knowing when to do something).

While PowerPoint, Google Slides, and Google Forms can do a lot of things, there are some obstacles that require more than they can handle, particularly if they involve variables, probabilities, or Boolean logic (using AND, OR, or NOT in choices). This is where you might want to consider using a spreadsheet like Excel, Numbers, or Google Sheets because they can take a player's input, process it, and produce different output in addition to being able to store a lot of data. In a spreadsheet, you can have players input strings of text or numbers and then write a formula to see if they match the answer. You can also use formulas to do complex calculations. Do not be fooled into thinking that spreadsheets only deal with numbers or that they are not very "GUI" (graphic user interface—basically, using pictures); you can turn the gridlines off and insert a picture. You can even enable it so that clicking on a cell with a picture does an action. I created an escape the room *Jotto* game (like *Wordle* except that the player only knows how many letters are the same in the guessed word as in the target word) in Excel by inserting a picture of an attic and having players guess the right three-letter word to unlock the trunk in the attic, which then allowed the player to unlock the attic door and then click on the hole (a black cell) which then opened up another Excel spreadsheet that put the player in a bedroom that required guessing a five-letter word to unlock that door (i.e., click a cell that linked to a third spreadsheet) to go down to the living room where they had to guess a seven-letter word, thus allowing players to "level up."

FIGURE 5.2 Excel Example of Jotto Word Game.

Repurposing common software tools to be game engines is easier than you would think!

Once you master co-opting software tools you are already familiar with to design games, you can delve into some tools that are specifically designed to create games (or you can skip a level and go directly to them!). There are lots of narrative branching tools that you can use to design an advanced *Choose Your Own Adventure* game. For example, *Twine* (twinery.org) is the free narrative branching tool that you played with in the previous chapter that allowed you to use variables and conditional statements. While I, and my students, have found that *Twine* has a "low floor" (easy onboarding) and "high ceiling" (allows you to do complicated things), there are other free narrative branching tools that have various levels of learning curves, such as *Inform7*, *Inklewriter*, *StoryMate*, and *TextAdventure*. By the time you read this, maybe there will be others! *Scratch* is a free block-based programming tool out of MIT that allows you to program lots of different types of games by dragging and dropping commands that are different shapes and fit together like puzzle pieces to create code. If a command doesn't fit within or below another command, then you know that those commands don't work together.

> **ACTION ITEM:** Go to https://scratch.mit.edu and try your hand at coding. Start with the orange event code that says, "When the green flag is clicked" and have Scratch the cat move 100 steps by dragging the move 10 steps underneath the "When the green flag is clicked" command and changing the 10 to 100. Then, keep playing around to see what you can do! If you feel ambitious, create your own game in *Scratch*!

Beyond these tools are other free game design engines such as *GameMaker*, *AdventureGameStudio*, and *KoduGameLab*. There may be others and, hopefully, even more coming out! In fact, there are some that are free, like *Unreal Engine* and *Unity*, that are used to design commercial off-the-shelf (COTS) games like *Fortnite* and *Among Us*!

Conclusion

Sylvester (2013) reminds us of why conflict is so appealing and why it needs to be such that it reveals who the playable character is:

> We're particularly interested in the struggles of others because it is only during conflict that a person's inner values and abilities are revealed. The more intense the conflict they face, the deeper we see into their true nature. We snore as our hero is forced to choose between skim and whole milk. Force him to choose between his wife's life and his own, and we stare, wondering who this man will show himself to be.
>
> (p. 22)

As you are picking up, the way these chapters are laid out are artificial distinctions as every aspect impacts the others. In the game introduction at the beginning of this chapter, the *but* is missing information, thus leading to the "so", or core game mechanic, of figuring it out, in this case, by using morphemic analysis to fill in the blanks on the pages. Going back and forth between these different aspects of your game design as creating and/or changing one impacts all others is exactly what iterative design is all about.

Chapter 5 Worksheet: Obstacles

Directions: Fill in the shapes below by describing each of the items. Add more obstacles as needed.

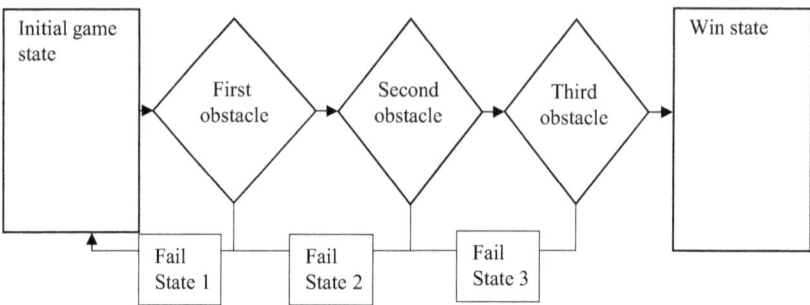

FIGURE 5.3 Game Flowchart.

Notes

1. My confession is that this mostly consisted of me watching my children play this game, although, weirdly, I was particularly good with the clawshot so they would let me play those sequences.
2. Theme songs for your game can really help set the mood! The game described at the beginning of this chapter had the perfect magically spooky song playing, which made me want to investigate more. When I played the first *Myst* game, just hearing the music got me excited. I'm sure there are movie theme songs that do the same for you (for me, this includes the Harry Potter theme song and *Star Wars*). In fact, familiar theme songs can be a good way of evoking certain moods. As long as you don't make your game publicly available and definitely don't monetize it or rob someone else of the profits (i.e., don't copy a whole book or game!), the TEACH Act (2002) allows teachers to use copyrighted material in their teaching.
3. GIFs assign colors to blocks of pixels and so are better for items that do not need to be photorealistic. They also have smaller file sizes than JPEG files because saying this 5 by 8 section of pixels needs to be black takes up less space than assigning each of those 40 pixels a color like JPEGs do. However, PNGs support transparent backgrounds, making them ideal to use as sprites (objects that move around in a game).

References

Anderson, L. W., & Krathwohl, D. R. (Eds.). (2001). *A taxonomy for learning, teaching and assessing: A revision of Bloom's Taxonomy of educational objectives: Complete edition*. New York: Longman.

Bartle, R. (1996/2006). Hearts, clubs, diamonds, spades: Players who suit MUDs. In K. Salen & E. Zimmerman (Eds.), *The game designer reader: A rules of play anthology* (pp. 754–787) Cambridge, MA: MIT Press.

Boller, S. & Kapp, K. (2017). *Play to learn: Everything you need to know about designing effective learning games*. Alexandria, VA: ATD Press.

Dille, F. & Platten, J. S. (2007). *The Ultimate guide to videogame writing and design*. New York, NY: Lone Eagle Publishing Company.

Gee, J. P. (2007). *Good videogames + good learning: Collected essays on videogames, learning, and literacy*. New York: Peter Lang.

McGonigal, J. (2011). *Reality is broken: Why games make us better and how they can change the world*. London: Penguin Books.

Miller, M. (2019). *Radagast the Brown and The Noble Quest to Save Mirkwood. Game created for EDC G 634 Introduction to Game-based Teaching taught by* J. Kellinger at Boston, MA: UMass Boston.

Prensky, M. (2011). Comments on research comparing games to other instructional methods. In S. Tobias and J. D. Fletcher (Eds.), *Computer games and instruction* (pp. 251–280). Charlotte, NC: Information Age Publishers.

Rabin, S. (2009). *Introduction to game development* (2nd ed.). Herndon, VA: Cengage Learning.

Robinett, W. (1984/2006). Adventure as a videogame: Adventure for the Atari 2600 from inventing the adventure game. In K. Salen & E. Zimmerman (Eds.), *The game designer reader: A rules of play anthology* (pp. 690–713) Cambridge, MA: MIT Press.

Schell, J. (2008). *The art of game design: A book of lenses*. Burlington, MA: Morgan Kaufmann.

Swan, R. (2010). Feedforward as an essential active principle of engagement in computer games. In R. Van Eck (Ed.), *Gaming and cognition: Theories and practice from the learning sciences* (pp. 108–136). Hershey, PA: Information Science Reference.

Sylvester, T. (2013). *Designing games: A guide to engineering experiences.* Sebastopol, CA: O'Reilly Media.

6

Implementing the Core Game Mechanic (So)

Hi, Mr. Fitz! It's your former student, Asya…

We're in DANGER and I need your students' HELP!

Captured from NASA by evil organization, the Thanosites… forced to write code to arm weapons throughout the world. Explode in 1 week.

*Left you a map. Follow it to disarm. Must fall in hands with **coordinate geometry expertise**, but hands they'd never suspect. Your class fits both!*

I had to carefully conceal the clues—couldn't risk captors figuring out what they mean before you do.

You are our greatest hope at stopping this attack before detonation! I know you can do it. Good luck!

(Sam Fitzgerald, *Ticking Time Bomb*, 2020)

This excerpt provides the backstory that explains why everything has to be so secretive in the coordinate geometry game mentioned previously. You can see from this "email" that the teacher receives, there are several story and game elements that make this game-story particularly compelling. First of all, the "Somebodies" are familiar—a letter from a former student to these students' current teacher. Second of all, the "Wanted," or the goal, is a big one—to save the world! Third of all, the "But" introduces a time element ("before detonation") that does what Sylvester (2013) describes—induces all the physical aspects of stress (increased heart rate, shallow breathing, etc.)—and then attaches the story elements to this to get students to feel excited and a little nervous. What is most important for this chapter, though, is this game's "So"—the core game mechanic of using coordinate geometry to save the day. This game levels up—the equations get harder and harder—in order to master the skill of solving these coordinate geometry equations by using a game as a "deliberate practice machine" (Koster, 2014, p. 100). James Gee (2007) calls designing one type of challenge in a way that lays the foundation for adding a layer of complexity to the next, creating "well-ordered problems" (p. 35). However, what this student of mine cleverly did is he provided scaffolding in the form of a help button to get to a cheat sheet the teacher in this scenario had created that explains how to do the different levels of problems. This helps provide the level of scaffolding students need to figure out the problem they are working on instead of assuming they will know it on their own. What I have found is that when doing regular homework assignments, students rely on the scaffolding I provided, but when they are playing a game, they only seek out help when they are truly stuck, and even then, they hesitate to do so. Others have found that as well: "[P]layers instinctively seek out the least amount of help necessary to advance them through the game, intuitively implementing a scaffolding approach to keep themselves in the ZPD" (Van Eck, 2007, p. 288). Notice, too, that the scaffolding is in keeping with the game. It is realistic to think that a teacher has actually created a cheat sheet with explanations for students studying coordinate geometry. One thing I want you to take away from this book is when creating these story-based immersive games, relate everything to the game-story; otherwise, you shatter that suspension of disbelief.

What Are Some Ways to Design Various Core Game Mechanics?

Dille and Platten (2007) point out that if someone is telling you a long-winded story and your mind has drifted off, as soon as the storyteller says, "Guess what?" (p. 40), your mind returns to the story. In other words, as soon as they ask you to "play" the story by playing a guessing game, your attention perks up. The more students "play" the game-story versus watching cutscenes, which are short videos in a video game, or reading, the more engaged they are. That being said, as long as the videos and the text have to do directly with the playing, i.e., whatever decision-making is at hand, players' minds are still engaged. As Sylvester (2013) notes, "Many media can provoke emotion through spectacle, character, or music; only games can do it through decision" (p. 120). Letting players know that a decision is forthcoming before providing the backstory, or introducing the conflict, or providing information will make it more likely that players pay attention. On the other hand, having players realize they need to come back to information when they need it can provide a sense of accomplishment and ownership over learning. I did this in the Romeo and Juliet game I described previously, when players find various books they only later realize they need in order to solve the different puzzles. "Display[ing] it," as Dille and Platten (2007) advise, allows players to actively construct meaning.

The trick to figuring out how much reading and viewing to offer the player is to give the player just the right amount of information so that the decisions do not feel arbitrary OR obvious. Sylvester (2013) observes, "The same decision can be made incomprehensible with too little information, fascinating with just the right amount of information, and trivial with too much information" (p. 127). In other words, you need to follow the "Goldilocks"[1] rule—not too much and not too little information. If the player does not have enough information to make a decision, they will make random choices and feel powerless in the end. If the player knows the consequences of the decisions and it is obvious which one will be the successful one, the game is no longer fun and, some would argue, no longer a game. Sylvester (2013) sums this up: "When we want a decision to be meaningful, its outcomes must be neither unknowable nor inevitable. They must be partially predictable" (p. 123). It is this "partial predictability" that leads to student learning and, interestingly, also what active readers do when they read stories. In fact, active readers, as well as active gameplayers, constantly tweak and revise their predictions as they receive more information (Jackson, 2009).

When students take tests, they are expected to know everything; otherwise, they get marked wrong and rarely do they get to try again. In games, players should not know for sure the outcomes of their decisions; otherwise, there is no element of "playing" a game—testing something out, seeing what happens, and making revisions. In other words, in order for an activity to be considered a game, there needs to be uncertainty. As Sylvester (2013) states, to create suspense, "the possibility of success must be real—and so must the possibility of failure" (p. 78). Miller (2004) points out,

> The most interesting gameplay arises from rules that have both positive and negative consequences. This means that the player must make decisions that are not always clear and automatic. Good gameplay, in effect, arises when choices are non-obvious and the player must explore different tactics to see what the trade-offs are for each decision.
> (Quoted in Mayra, 2008, p. 16)

When a player makes decisions where each choice has pros and cons, the values of the player, or really of the player as the main character, are revealed. These kinds of decisions are called judgment calls and are essential in games about ethical and moral decision-making.

Sometimes, however, we might want to design games, or at least some game decisions, where there is one right answer, particularly in subject areas where answers are more clear-cut. These kinds of decisions are called puzzles. While there are lots of different kinds of puzzles, Sylvester (2013) contends, "Good game decisions, including good puzzles, are always based around nonobvious uses of mechanics that work in obvious ways. And when [the player] sees the solution, [they] will know it immediately and fill with a rush of insight" (pp. 136–137). For me, this happened when I was playing *Myst* and could not figure out what to do next. Finally, at a loss, I did the only thing I had not done—which was to close the doors to the cave from the inside. When I did so, two passageways that were behind the doors when they were open were revealed. This insight actually came into play in real life when I stayed at a friend's condo for the first time and could not figure out why the outside of the building was larger than the interior space. I thought about this *Myst* incident and closed the front door while inside the condo, which revealed the doorway to the main bedroom. My students have often expressed these feelings of insight when solving puzzles in my game-based courses, so much so that in one of my presentations, I use the surprise emoji to show what my students look like when they get it. Often, however, it happens not in my presence but after they step away. My students have told me that, after pausing working on one of the game challenges, they will have a "flash of insight" where something "clicks in their brain," with some saying that it was "so simple" they didn't know why it took them so long to figure it out. Those "duh!" moments are the ones that stick with us. Finding that "just right" amount of information so that students productively struggle and then have that "rush of insight" is key to designing good puzzles.

In order to make sure these puzzles do not end up feeling like a worksheet or a test dressed up as a game, it is imperative to make sure they are embedded in or, better yet, advance the storyline. Boller and Kapp (2017) list several ways to do this depending on your goals, including

- "race to the finish" games, which are good for situations with time constraints;
- acquiring territory, which is good for gaining knowledge, particularly if you use the "display it" tactic;
- exploration, which is good for comparison/contrast skills;
- collecting and sorting items, which can teach categorization;
- matching items, which is good for learning associations;
- alignment is good for ordering information;
- rescuing someone or escaping a situation can be dependent upon recalling some vital piece of information;
- outwitting someone or figuring out a solution to a puzzle, such as a locking mechanism is good for problem-solving skills; and
- constructing, building, or creating something is good for applying and synthesizing knowledge (pp. 50–51).

In fact, Boller and Kapp (2017) point out that combining two of these, particularly if they are opposed to each other, such as racing to the finish and building something, can really increase the challenge. Koster (2014) adds a few more, such as timing (like when jumping or swinging from rope to rope), resource management, aiming, fitting things together, and understanding odds and probability, and concludes that all of these have to do with identifying patterns, something humans are primed to do in order to survive. But you do need to make sure that puzzles are solvable and do not "take advantage of the player or make the player feel stupid" (Bond, 2018, p. 219). I always try to provide positive encouragement when students are struggling to figure something out and to notice and congratulate them when they do.

Remember, though, to focus the challenges on what you want students to learn. Don't make players learn something new unless it is related to the learning objective. For example, I remember a professional development I attended where the presenter was so excited about this "learning stick" with different yarn items on it that students were supposed to associate with letters of the alphabet. However, the different items had nothing to do with the letters; they just added an extra layer of learning for the students. There is a reason that "a is for apple" works because not only does the word apple start with the letter "a" and the "a" sound, but it looks like an "a." Having students learn something unrelated to the learning goal will make students, and you, feel like they are wasting their time. This includes the directions:

> You don't want your players to spend valuable time figuring out the game. Rules that are too cumbersome can lead to cognitive overload, and players will be learning only how to play the game and not the desired instructional goal. Gameplay that is too complex will frustrate learners and distract them from the learning they need to do.
>
> (Sylvester, 2013, p. 25)

You might have some activities that are indirectly related to the learning goals or just tangentially so. If you use a metaphor, make that clear, at least in the debriefing sessions. If it is a fun story-related challenge but not focused on the central skill, make it an optional mini-game. I do this in my coding class—there are optional mini-games whenever a player levels up that are related to the storyline but not essential to following the storyline and that do not require players to use the core game mechanic or the "So" of the story, which is coding. Students report that they enjoy these "breaks" as rewards for reaching the next level. However, what students don't always realize at the time is that these mini-games also involve "stealth" learning, as they provide examples for their final project. I make this explicit in the instructions for their final project when I encourage students to go back to those mini-games as inspiration for their final projects and to look at the coding to see how certain actions are accomplished.

Once you have determined the core game mechanic and how that skill will be played in the game (the "So" of the story), you need to think about how to do so in a way that students can "level up." In other words, each iteration of enacting that skill needs to get increasingly more difficult. A good example of a game with "well-ordered problems" (Gee, 2007, p. 35) was one my student called "Moving up the ranks," where the player starts off as a medical intern who encounters increasingly more and more difficult-to-diagnose patients. If students do not get better through practice and the harder challenges do not discriminate between players who have more experience, then you need to revamp those challenges. This can involve challenges that require more information, making the challenges more complex, adding a new concept or skill, or changing the conditions. One way you can structure these challenges is to start off with declarative knowledge, the *what*, i.e., knowing facts, and then move on to procedural knowledge or understanding *how* to perform skills and then moving on to conditional knowledge, i.e., learning *when* to apply knowledge or skills in which situations. I did this in my data-based planning class where students had to demonstrate knowledge of the *what* during the interview process, had to apply that what to show the *how* in using data from a diagnostic assessment to create an action plan, and then show they knew the *when* to apply certain knowledge in order to redeem a colleague who had been accused of helping his students cheat on a standardized test. You have done this too! This is how the practice game, *Newbie Adventure in Three Acts*, was structured in the previous chapter. Just like you design your curriculum to increase in difficulty, so should the challenges in your curricular game.

What Are Some Ways to Provide Scaffolding?

The trick with teaching is that different students need different amounts and different pieces of information in order to put the pieces together in their minds. In other words, the constant teaching task of differentiation. In game design terminology, this is called keeping players in the flow zone. This is where games can really shine. Because failure is a feature of games, you can layer information so that students can try something just by having a little bit of information, and if, they do not get it at first, with each attempt you can provide a little bit more information until they get it. Sometimes this involves having the information available but not obvious and drawing attention to it if players do not solve the problem right away. Other times it involves providing hints that are more and more detailed and are triggered by certain lapses of time or a certain number of attempts. For example, an NPC can say, "I wonder what would happen if you tried this?" or "Do you remember when this other similar thing happened?" Having an NPC who does not trust the main character at first and so gives very little information, but as they see the playable character earnestly try and fail, this earns their trust so they are willing to divulge more might be a good in-game way to do this. You could even have the NPC demonstrate the skill for the player to observe and copy, with each iteration slowing down or zooming in on what part needs improvement, or the opposite—viewing an NPC fail and seeing the consequences. Layering the feedback so it becomes closer and closer to hand-holding the more students struggle can adapt a game to each individual student's needs. On the other hand, providing less and less scaffolding would be a way to level up the challenges in your game.

Another advantage of games is that players can advance at their own pace and therefore can rush through (or "speed-running" as gamers call it) material they already understand until they get to a point where they need to slow down and process the material. Because you will create your game with a string of increasingly harder challenges, you can replicate this as well. In these linear-type games, allowing players to skip ahead if they pass an assessment can help keep players engaged, particularly if it is a game that students replay. This can be particularly useful at the beginning of a game and can be couched as "training," but you can also have optional practice areas throughout, an aspect of my coding class that students have praised. My own children were excited when an assessment tool used in their school added the ability to skip the introduction and explanations since they were tired of having to sit through material they already knew. However, in your game, you do not want students to be able to skip over essential information. One way to combat this is to require students to view or read it once and then give them the option to skip over it if they encounter it again or to test out of having to go through it (always, though, with something that makes sense in the game-story). You can also make some nonessential information skippable.

If you design a *Choose Your Own Adventure*–type game with lots of branches, you do need to make sure that, no matter which paths students choose, they still get all the core essential information they need. One way to do this is to "foldback" the decision tree so students have to come back to the core game experience, either through choices leading back or encountering dead ends and having to retreat. Crawford (2013) uses the term "foldback with a boost" (p. 123) to describe requiring players to explore both decision choices to move on. He provides an example of choosing one cave direction as ending in a dead-end, but in that dead-end is a sleeping potion needed to put the dragon that is guarding the treasure in the other cave direction to sleep. However you design your curricular game, enabling students to move at their own pace keeps them in their flow zone, as they can spend more time on areas where they struggle and cruise through areas they don't.

There may be cases where you want students to play your curricular game and move forward, or not, as a whole class. This has lots of advantages, particularly if you require a majority or unanimous vote for every decision because then students have to explain their reasoning for their decisions in order to convince others. This not only allows students to learn different strategies and ways of thinking from each other, but it also gives you, the teacher, a way to assess student understanding and to document growth. The danger of this, however, is that you could have just a few students dominate, and others remain silent or, worse, give up. In order to avoid this, you could have some way of surveying what individual students want to do and then reporting out the overall results such as by using the "Poll Everywhere" app. You could also do something much more analog. You can put a number in each corner of your room and then number the options of every decision and have students physically go to the corner with the number of the option they would choose. They can then consult with the other students in their corner and report out their collective reasoning to try to convince others to come to their corner. The game doesn't move on until a consensus is reached. Students then go back to the "neutral zone"—the middle of the classroom—to await the next decision. This has the advantage of easily adding a physical dimension to your game as well. Having students fill out anonymous exit tickets at the end of each day can give you a glimpse into how the class dynamics are working to make sure that a student isn't feeling like their input is being ignored.

As educators, we know that one of the best means of scaffolding is feedback. We also know that there are lots of different types of feedback: letting a student know if something is right or wrong, pointing a student to a particular area where something is wrong and letting them figure out what it is, explaining why something is wrong, and telling a student how to correct a mistake. Games do the same things. Lack of success lets players know they need to do something differently. Sometimes this comes with an indication of where that change needs to happen, such as zooming in on something, making a noise, or having something blink. Sometimes an NPC or even a physical sign will indicate why something is wrong or even how to correct it. Sometimes this might be giving the player feedback about how much success they have achieved, such as an increase or decrease in health or energy or the percentage match to the correct answer. Whatever that feedback is and however it is given, it is the driver of the learning in the attempt, feedback, revision, try again process.

Players need to know both when they got something right by being rewarded and when they got something wrong by being "punished"—whether that be by lack of progress, regression, or removal of resources. According to brain science, being rewarded sparks neurotransmitters in the brain that help cement learning (Doidge, 2007, p. 71), which is why it is important that rewards are reserved for making progress on the core game mechanic skill, the "So" of the game-story. Points, praise from an NPC, new abilities, new resources, new information, new areas to explore all reward the player, but, like everything, you need to make sure they are in keeping with the game's theme. Movement on a progress bar (something that shows a player how far they are in a game) is very rewarding—but only if they can see how much they have left to go. I learned this the hard way when I designed a bookshelf in one of my online classes where a new book would show up every time students completed a level. I thought this would be inspiring until a student told me she groaned every time a new book showed up on the bookshelf because it meant more work. This taught me two things: (1) I needed to make my class more fun and (2) that, unless you have something that indicates how much is left (e.g., the undone books grayed out or with a lock on them), students don't feel like they are making progress toward an end goal, instead progress feels endless. While a syllabus will usually show all the modules, aka levels, because syllabi are typically organized around the passage of time—something not under a player's control—they are a poor substitute for a progress bar unless they are designed as such.

When a player makes a mistake, the best "punishments" are the natural consequences of their actions. For example, if the player uses the informal "you" when addressing an NPC of higher status when speaking French, the NPC could respond indignantly, "I am not your friend!" Make sure you are punishing behaviors you want to discourage. As Salen and Zimmerman (2004) point out, if an explosion happens because a player pushes a random button, you are punishing curiosity (p. 367). Having NPCs ask questions like, "Why do you think that happened? What might happen if…? What do you think that is over there? Does this remind you of anything? Who do you think you could ask about this?" can prompt the reflection needed for learning in the feedback cycle. Couching the failure feedback as praise can help inspire confidence with statements like, "You don't usually make that mistake," or "You almost always win!" Replaying the player's actions can help them pinpoint what went wrong. Even wait time is scaffolding as it gives the player a chance to figure it out on their own. I cannot count how many times I have gotten a "never mind" email after a student, or sometimes even a colleague, has asked me how to do something and I didn't respond right away. An immediate response would have fostered dependency and superficial learning; a delayed response can foster self-sufficiency and deeper learning (Kapur & Bielaczyc, 2012). This pairs well with exit tickets, homework reflections, and in-game journals, letters, etc., where players can reflect on their decisions, their impact, and alternatives. In some of my courses, I use what I call "delayed gradification," where students move forward just by turning in an assignment, but their progress is blocked later on if they don't get a passing grade on that assignment. By giving myself time to grade their work, students' progress is not halted by waiting for me to grade something but rather by their own abilities. Whatever you do, though, you want to make sure the player does not blame the game, which happens when things feel arbitrary, so make it clear that the player has agency to change their own behavior with progressive disclosure about how they should do so.

I have found that the best scaffolding is you, the teacher! The optimal way to do this is to be an NPC in the game-story, usually by playing a wise mentor type of role. For example, in my coding class, students can reach out to "Frank" if they need a quick answer or "Tory" if they need further explanation. However, both links lead to my email address, and I respond accordingly. You can also just be the teacher reaching out to students when you see they need help, checking in frequently, and making sure they know you are there if they get stuck. Students have expressed appreciation for me being proactive in checking in with them both when they are stuck and when they have success. One student emailed me on Mother's Day to thank me for being a "mother" to all the students in the class. As their teacher, you have a good sense of exactly how much pushing a particular student needs; what information to provide, including providing analogies with an interest of theirs; and when to let a student struggle a little bit longer; you yourself are the perfect scaffolding.

Be mindful of how that feedback operates. For one thing, feedback needs to be consistent. If trying to open a door elicits a jingling sound indicating the player needs to find a key to open it, do not then have another door handle jingle when it is a door that does not open at all. Rewards also need to be in keeping with the story. In the first iteration of my coding class, I created a "Bonus Shop" where students could accumulate bonus points and "buy" different items, such as a deadline extension or extra credit points. Then I realized that a bonus shop makes no sense in the context of a game where the protagonist is tied up in their office practically the whole time, so I got rid of it. Another consideration is the message that rewards send. For example, if a reward is a homework pass, that sends the message that homework is not important and something to avoid. Extrinsic rewards, rewards that do not have to do with the game-story, such as badges, should be used sparingly, if at all, because they "can displace and even destroy the intrinsic fulfillment of play" (Sylvester, 2013, p. 212). If they are used, they should be used for boring, repetitive tasks, what gamers call grinding. Instead of using extrinsic rewards, create intrinsic ones by embedding them in the game-story itself. For example, instead of external badges, the player's avatar could receive an accessory that signifies achieving a certain skill, which could be an actual badge if that makes sense story-wise or an item that allows the playable character to be more powerful or some sort of resource such as money, health, time, or fuel, or a new piece of information, or entrance to a whole new section of the world with, of course, harder challenges or, most commonly, unlocking the next story segment. In the same vein, "punishment" for a mistake should be in keeping with the game-story as well. This could involve a setback—going to an earlier point in the game—or a timeout where the player cannot try again until a certain amount of time has elapsed or a degradation of skills or resources, or simply just not being able to move forward in the game-story until success is achieved. In some instances, death—of the playable character or the patient they are trying to save or the creature the player is attempting to rescue, etc.—might make the most sense in the context of the game-story. In that case, allow players to restart the game but also allow them to skip the introduction or certain cutscenes so they don't get too frustrated. Whatever you decide, make sure it makes the most sense in terms of both the game-story AND the learning goals. While your game-story does not have to be realistic, it does need to be both coherent and plausible in order to be believable.

What Are Some Ways to Measure and Assess Success?

One of our jobs as teachers, at least the way our current educational system works, is to grade students. This involves assessing how successful students are at achieving the learning objectives we set for them and conveying that to students and their caregivers. Remember earlier when I warned against overcomplicating the game, including the instructions, by making students learn something unrelated to your learning goals? That also applies to grading. I learned this the hard way. When I was a beginning high school English teacher, I set up my grading system to have weighted grades so that homework was worth a certain percentage, quizzes a higher percentage, and so forth. My thinking, as an English teacher, was that this system would also reinforce what they were learning in math class. Instead it just confused and frustrated students and parents. On the advice of a guidance counselor, I then changed my grading system to points. This was much cleaner and did not distract from the learning in my English classes. In fact, one of my more successful final projects was in my poetry unit, where I clearly laid out how many points each activity was worth and students could then choose what and how much they did, essentially determining their own grade. Initially, students' final grades in my classes were determined by dividing the number of points they earned by the number of points possible. I then streamlined my point system, making everything (except extra credit points) add up to 100 points, thus making it easy for students to see where they fall letter grade-wise.

An even easier way to grade students is based on their progress—i.e., how many levels they have completed. One of my students created a game where the player worked their way up through the different levels of a hospital, from the ER to the ICU, by diagnosing different patients. She didn't need to "score" players: a player succeeded if a patient got healthy and failed if a patient died. If the player made it to the top level (or the top rank), she knew they had done "A" work, the second to the top level was "B" work, and so on. Many of my courses are designed this way—getting to the end means getting an A, the level prior a B, and so forth. Some of my classes use a "river and lakes" approach (also known as "string of pearls") where each level has several tasks that students can complete in any order, but they must be successful in all of them by earning enough points to move to the next level. If you use this approach in an in-person class, you can have learning stations set up around the room. In some of my classes, getting to right before the end—before the final boss battle—gets them around a B and only after being scored on the boss battle, usually a final project like creating a game or designing a curricular unit plan, can they get to an A. Because everything in my courses (except bonus points) are revise and resubmit, students actually *choose* their final grade. If the final project earns them a B+ in the course, they can keep that B+ or incorporate my feedback to revise and resubmit and work their way up to an A. If students have to earn a certain number of points or pass a quiz or solve a puzzle in order to move forward in your curricular game, then you have to have retakes; otherwise, students will get stuck with nowhere to go. Take advantage of those retakes to provide feedback to help students improve.

Another way to assess students is to use adaptive branching to adjust to students' skill levels and then see where each student ends up. There are many ways you can devise adaptive branching but I find the most effective is to actually start with the intermediate level. If a student gets it right, they branch to a harder level. If a student gets it wrong, they branch to a lower level. You then continue from there. However, you may want to begin with a lower-level question and have students work their way up or not. Adaptive branching also allows you, as the teacher, to mold the scaffolding to a student's individual level. A tool that can help you automate this is Google Forms.

> **ACTION ITEM:** Because the purpose of this action item is to introduce you to adaptive branching in Google Forms, we are going to base it on one of your existing multiple-choice tests or quizzes instead of creating something new. From your multiple-choice test, identify three different

levels of questions on the same topic or skill. Then, open Google Forms. Put in the intermediate-level question as the first item. Then create a new section by clicking on the equal sign on the right-hand side and put the beginning level question. Do the same for the advanced level question. Go back to the first question, select the three vertical dots in the lower right-hand corner, and choose "Go to section based on answer," like we did for the practice game previously. You will see that each option now has a drop-down menu. Select the advanced level question section to go to for the correct answer and the beginning level question for all the wrong answers. If you are thinking that this action item feels familiar, you would be correct! This is the exact same thing we did to create a basic *Choose Your Own Adventure* story by answering the question "Should you say yes or should you say no?" in the Somebody chapter. You can keep going for as long as you want. Be sure to test it out to make sure it works by using the Preview feature.

If you choose to use adaptive branching to adjust to students' skill levels, I recommend drawing out a flow chart first. Branching like this is a great way to fine-tune your evaluations of students and to provide targeted support and feedback, but keeping track of all the links can get complicated fast. However, the benefits outweigh the difficulty, particularly if you use this method to provide feedback based on the individual incorrect answers students choose, tailoring your game even more to each student.

While adaptive branching like this is good for puzzles, it is not so good for judgment calls unless you devise ways to make students' thinking visible or audible, not only because it helps you assess students and provide feedback but also because it helps students clarify their thinking and exposes students to multiple perspectives. I discussed earlier how whole-class decision-making via four corners can make this happen. Breaking students into small groups and visiting them frequently is another way to do this. Having students fill out decision trees or using exit tickets helps; however, a better option is to have students use a reflection tool that is in keeping with the game. For example, students can keep a "field journal" if they are a scientist or a diary or journal if they are a historical or literary figure or write a letter to an NPC or a letter to the editor or whatever makes sense in the context of the game-story. That way, reflection is part of the game itself—and players can do it in character.

I have read some books and articles that advocate for leaderboards as a way to motivate students. I did try a leaderboard in one of my classes but quickly found that, while it motivated the top three students to jockey for first place, it ended up discouraging the rest of the class, so I quickly abandoned it. Instead, I periodically send emails to the top students in the class to let them know where they stand. Boller and Kapp (2017) suggest only setting students up for competition with each other for boring, repetitive tasks and to use achievements, rewards, and feedback to encourage cooperation and teamwork for tasks that involve critical thinking, creativity, and judgment calls. However, there is a way to encourage both cooperation and competition by having small groups compete against each other. Doing this then diffuses the pain of being in last place while still rewarding those in first place.

> **PRACTICE GAME: Leveling Up** For this practice game, we are going to go back to *Scratch*, the free block-based programming language I had you play around with previously. I'm going to have you create a catching game with levels that get increasingly harder. To do so, you will need to choose a background (mouseover the icon at the bottom of the Stage box, select the magnifying glass, and then click on a background) and two sprites—one to be the catcher and one to be caught that will copy itself and drop from the sky (mouseover the catface icon in the sprite section, click

the magnifying glass, and choose a sprite). You can choose strategically so it tells a story, or even goes along with the overall game-story you are creating, or just choose randomly and use this exercise just to get more practice with *Scratch*. In the upper-right-hand window, drag the catcher sprite to the bottom of the window and the other sprite to the top. Go to variables, Make New Variable, and create one called timer and another one called score.

Now that you have set things up, I am going to use the same distinctions I used before for directions, instructions, and visual aids: directions to tell you what to do, instructions to tell you how to do it, and a visual aid to show you. I want you to first try figuring out what to do based on the directions. If you need more help, you can follow the instructions. If you need to, you can view the visual aid or just use the visual aid to check your work. *Please note that software tools can change, so these instructions and visuals are as of the writing of this book.*

Catcher Directions: Code the catcher sprite so pressing on the left button makes it move left and the right button makes it move right. When the catcher catches an object falling from the sky, increase the score by one.

Catcher Instructions: Click on the sprite you chose to be the catcher and select the code tab. Click on Events and drag the "When Space [key pressed]" command to the empty coding area in the middle. Click on the word "Space" and select "left arrow" instead. Select Motion, then drag "move 10 steps" under the "When left arrow key pressed" command. Then change it to −10 steps by typing in the white oval. If your sprite has multiple costumes that are in various stages of walking (click the costumes tab), then select Looks and drag "next costume" under your list of commands in the coding window. Do the same for the "right arrow," except keep it at +10 steps. Now select Events and drag "When greenflag is clicked" and then select Variables and drag "set my variable to zero" but change "my variable" to "score" and place it under "When greenflag is clicked." Look in the Control commands and drag the Forever loop over, and within that, place the If/Then command. In the hexagon, drag "touching mousepointer" (located in the Sensing commands) but change mousepointer to the sprite that is going to fall from the sky. Within the If/then command, drag the "change my variable by one" command, which is located under variables. Then change "my variable" to "score." Test it out by clicking on the green flag and using the left and right arrows to move the catcher sprite.

Catcher Visual Aid:

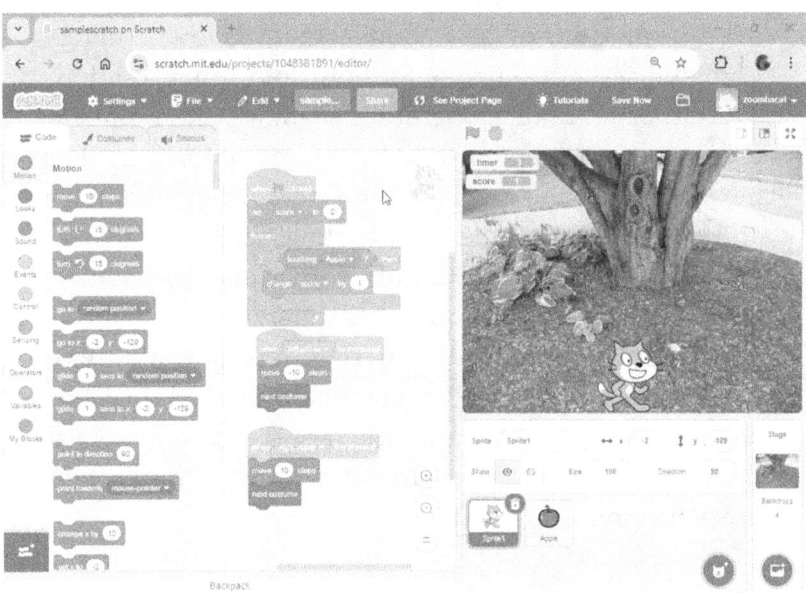

FIGURE 6.1 Scratch Example of Catcher Code.

Dropping Object Directions: Code the sprite you chose to fall to fall from the top of the screen in random places for ten seconds.

Dropping Object Instructions: Now click on the sprite you chose to fall from the sky and select the code tab. Drag the "When greenflag is clicked" command (under Events) and put the "hide" command from Looks under that. Then, from the Variables commands, drag the "set my variable to zero" command (changing "my variable" to "timer") and drag the "repeat until" command located under Control. In the hexagon, drag the green command that has a blank oval = 50 from Operators. Change the 50 to 10 and go to variables, and drag the timer variable into the first oval. Within the "repeat until" command, drag these three commands: "wait one seconds" (from Control), "change 'timer' by one" (from Variables), and "create a clone of myself" (from Control). Then, drag "When I start as a clone" over from Control and, under that, "show" (under Looks), "set x to" (from Motion) and "pick random −220 to 220" (under Operators changing the numbers to these), and "repeat until" (under Control). In that hexagon, drag the green "or" hexagon from Operators and, in one of those hexagons, "touching 'the catcher' sprite" from Sensing and in the other one, "y position <−157" (using the < from Operators and the "y position" from Motion). Within that repeat until loop, place the "change y by 10" command from Motion but change the 10 to −10. Under the repeat until loop, place the "delete this clone" command from Control. Now press the green flag and try it.

Dropping Object Visual Aid:

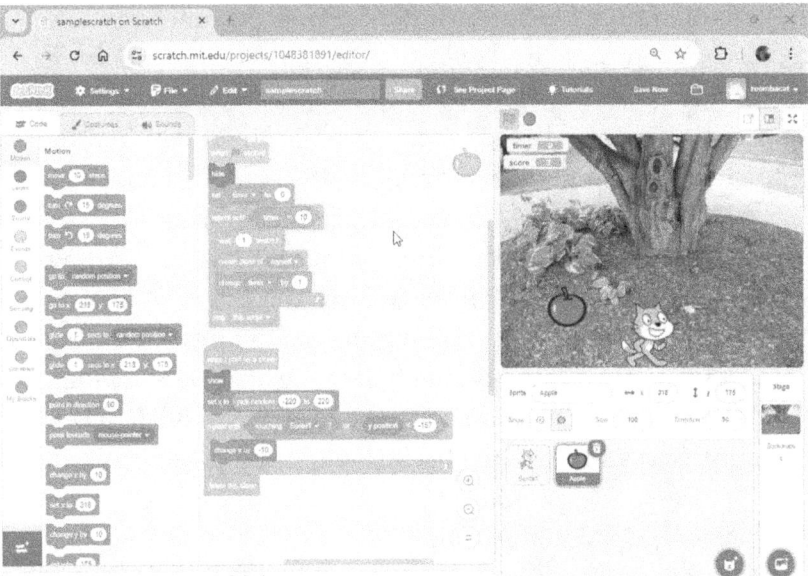

FIGURE 6.2 Scratch Example of Falling Object Code.

Leveling Up Directions: Choose three new backgrounds—one for losing, one for the next level, and one for winning the game. Set it so the losing background is displayed if the catcher catches five or fewer objects, and the next level background is displayed if the catcher catches more than five. Design that level the same as the first level, except that the catcher only has 8 seconds and has to catch a total of 15 items (including the items caught on the first level). If the catcher does so, display the winning background.

Leveling Up Instructions: Once you get that level working, create a new level by choosing or designing three new backgrounds—one for losing, one for the next level, and one for winning. Click on the word stage and make sure the code tab is selected. Drag the "When green flag is clicked" command from Control to the coding window. Then, drag the "switch backdrop to …" from Looks and select the original backdrop. Drag the "wait until" command from Control and insert "timer = 10" by using the =

equation from Operators and dragging the timer variable over. Then add the "wait one second" command from Control below that. Drag the "If/then" command from Control over and place "score > 5" in the if hexagon by using the < operator and dragging the score variable over. Within the if section, drag "switch backdrop to…" from Looks and select the backdrop for the next level. Then drag "broadcast message1" from Events. You can change message1 to "level up" by clicking the down arrow, selecting "New message," and typing that in the box. Place "switch backdrop to…" from Looks in the Else part of the If/Then command and select the backdrop for losing.

Leveling Up Visual Aid 1 of 3:

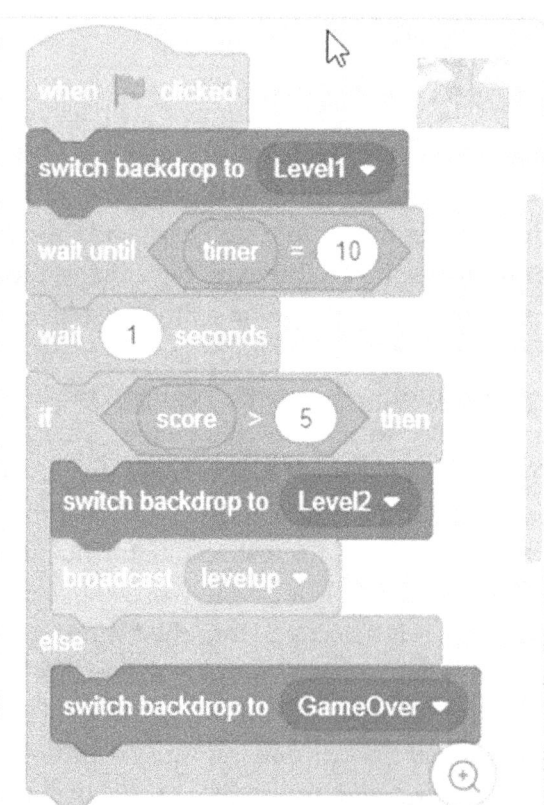

FIGURE 6.3 Scratch Example of Leveling Up Code for Backdrops.

Then, go to the falling object sprite, drag "when I receive 'level up'" from Events over, right-click the code under the "When green flag is clicked", choose "duplicate" and drag that copied code under "when I receive 'level up'". Change the number in the "repeat until timer = 10" to 8.

Leveling Up Visual Aid 2 of 3:

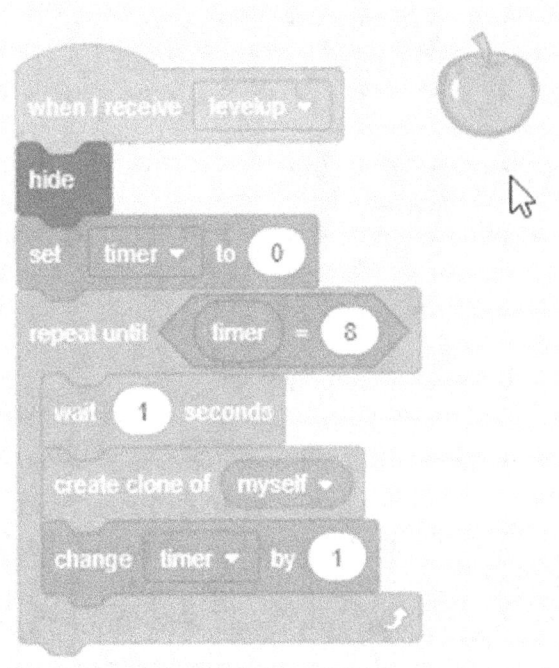

FIGURE 6.4 Scratch Example of Leveling Up Code for Falling Objects.

Go back to Stage and choose one final "You win" backdrop. Drag another "When greenflag is clicked" and a "forever" loop. Within that, drag "if score > 15" and insert "switch backdrop" to the "you win" backdrop and also then drag "stop all" under that. Now test it out.

Leveling Up Visual Aid 3 of 3:

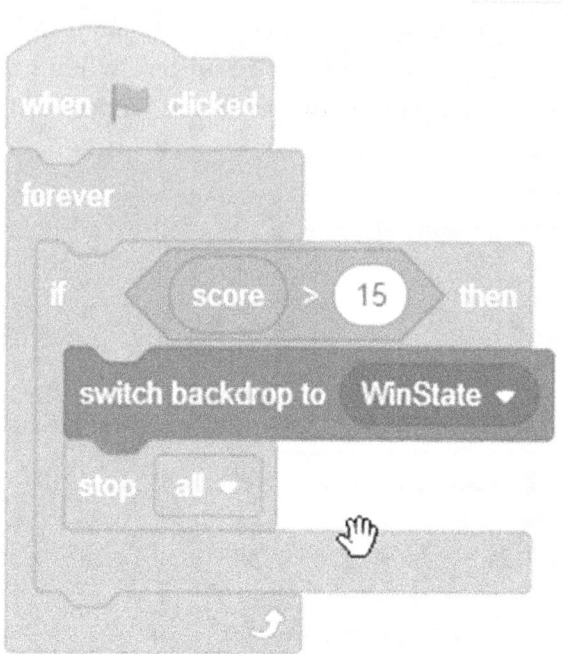

FIGURE 6.5 Scratch Example of Win-State Code.

Final set of directions: This is the most important part: make changes and test to see what happens. Try different things such as having the items fall faster or the catcher sprite follow the mousepointer. See what works for you and what doesn't. Add new levels. Play around with this as much as you want. This is where the true learning is. Not in following my directions but in the playing around and finding out.

In the previous practice game, following instructions and copying what I did wasn't learning; it was simply doing. Following just the directions and not looking at the instructions or the visual aids involved more figuring things out, but it was the last paragraph of playing around where you got to try something out, get feedback, and make adjustments, where real learning occurred. We have all probably had the experience of following GPS directions mindlessly and not really knowing how we got to our destination. In fact, if we were asked to find our way back without the GPS, we probably wouldn't be able to do so. But, when you figure out directions by looking at a map, you learn the landscape. In the earlier case, I provided a foundation from which you could then make changes and play around. In your learning game, get students started, but make sure you give them the freedom to fail and to try again. With each success, provide a new challenge with less scaffolding until they can do it on their own.

Conclusion

The crux of a story is how a protagonist manages to overcome the odds, defeat their enemies, and/or figure out a way to solve a problem. This is where skill development comes into play, the "So" of your game-story. Johnson (2013) remarks,

> Meaning emerges from the game's mechanics—the set of decisions and consequences unique to each one. What does a game ask of the player? What does it punish and what does it reward? What strategies and styles does the game encourage? Answering these questions reveals what a game is actually about.
> (Quoted in Rusch, 2017, p. 31)

The "So" is the learning objective of the curricular game. Make sure the challenges in your game require students to enact the "So" skill as the core game mechanic. If your game has students doing word searches, unless your core game mechanic is finding words among a bunch of letters, you need to change your challenges. Your game should provide lots of opportunities for students to practice the "so." Just like you "level up" your curricular units by creating lessons that build on each other, so should your game. The feedback the game gives provides scaffolding to help students get to the next level. By embedding this skill-building in a game-story, you give learning meaning, allow students to experience the curriculum, and ramp up their skills.

Chapter 6 Worksheet: Levels

Directions: Fill in the following chart by describing what performance at each of those levels looks like for your game's core game mechanic.

Core Game Mechanic:			
	Beginner	**Intermediate**	**Expert**
What this looks like			
Evidence of achieving level			
Game challenge that can produce that evidence			
How this fits in the story			

Note

1. Goldilocks is a story about a girl who finds a home where there are three sizes of everything to accommodate the three sizes of its occupants. For Goldilocks, one is always too big, one too little, and the middle one "just right."

References

Boller, S. & Kapp, K. (2017). *Play to learn: Everything you need to know about designing effective learning games*. Alexandria, VA: ATD Press.

Bond, J. (2018). *Introduction to game design, prototyping, and development*. Upper Saddle River, NJ: Addison-Wesley.

Crawford, C. (2013). *On interactive storytelling*. Berkeley, CA: New Riders.

Dille, F. & Platten, J. S. (2007). *The Ultimate guide to videogame writing and design*. New York, NY: Lone Eagle Publishing Company.

Doidge, N. (2007). *The Brain that changes itself*. New York: Penguin.

Fitzgerald, S. (2020). *Ticking time bomb*. Game created for EDC G 634 Introduction to Game-based Teaching taught by J. Kellinger at UMass Boston.

Gee, J. P. (2007). *Good videogames + good learning: Collected essays on videogames, learning, and literacy*. New York: Peter Lang.

Jackson, J. (2009). The reading-writing connection. In Flippo, R. & Caverly, D. (Eds.), *Handbook of college reading and study strategy research* (pp. 145–173). Mahwah, NJ: Lawrence Erlbaum Associates.

Johnson, S. (2013). What is your game actually about? *Gamasutra: The art and business of making games*. Retrieved 9/11/24 from https://www.gamedeveloper.com/design/what-is-your-game-actually-i-about-i-

Kapur, M. & Bielaczyc, K. (2012). Designing for productive failure. *Journal of the Learning Sciences, 21*(1), 45–83.

Koster, R. (2014). *A Theory of fun for game design*. Sebastopol, CA: O'Reilly Media.

Mayra, F. (2008). *An introduction to game studies*. Thousand Oaks, CA: Sage.

Miller, S. (2004). What is gameplay? In J. Newman, & I. Simons (Eds.), *Difficult questions about video games*. Nottingham, England: Suppose Books.

Salen, K. & Zimmerman, E. (2004). *Rules of play: Game design fundamentals*. Cambridge, MA: MIT Press.

Rusch, D. (2017). *Making deep games: Designing games with meaning and purpose*. Boca Raton, FL: CRC Press.

Sylvester, T. (2013). *Designing games: A guide to engineering experiences*. Sebastopol, CA: O'Reilly.

Van Eck, R. (2007). Building artificially intelligent learning games. In D. Gibson, C. Aldrich, & M. Prensky (Eds.), *Games and simulations in online learning: Research and development frameworks* (pp. 271–307). Hershey, PA: Information Science Publishing.

7

Orchestrating the End Game (Then)

As the intruders apply their torture device again, you start to fade. It's now or never. You figure your robot Sparky can't fight them, but maybe, just maybe, multiple robots can out-number them and wall them in until the police arrive. It defies the laws of physics, but does use logic, or rather, Object-Oriented Programming. You think "CREATE CLONE" really hard. Much to your amazement—and the amazement of the intruders—another robot appears.

You realize your mental faculties are fading so you won't be able to do this repeatedly. Instead **you'll need to program Sparky and his clone army to clone themselves in order to create a wall of robots to trap the intruders** *until the police arrive, but you suspect that if Sparky creates too many clones, the room won't be big enough for that many robots and they will all explode at once. As your consciousness fades, you make one last attempt to telepathically code Sparky.*

(Kellinger, *Coding for Non-Coders*, 2022)

For your curricular game we have talked about ramping up skills. This should conclude with a final challenge where the player needs to use all the skills acquired all at once to defeat the final boss, just like your curricular units often have a final test or project. In games, these are called Final Boss Battles. These are the climax of games and should be the climax of your game-story. In the previous case, students have to figure out how to code their robot Sparky to create just enough clones to trap the thieves but not so many that the room explodes. However, technically, students have to succeed in this boss battle to get to the actual boss battle—coding a videogame of their own. I find that for curricular games, having a final test of skills to demonstrate they have enough skill to go off and create something on their own can work really well. In the case of my coding class, this is the true "Then":

> *A few months later...*
> *Now that you are out of the hospital and have gone to the FBI, you find yourself feeling happier and freer than ever. You spend your days creating new games for Sparky.*
> *You think back to when you first started playing around with* Scratch. *You smile at yourself as you think of all the fun you had discovering how easy—and hard—it was to code. But it was, and still is, in the words of Jane McGonigal (2011), "hard fun."*
> (Kellinger, Coding for Non-Coders, 2022)

Students then get directions for their final project: designing a game of their own. Many students have cited this final project as their favorite part of the class because they enjoyed the freedom and creativity and, therefore, could pour their passion into it. When a student used the phrase "excruciatingly fun" to describe troubleshooting his final project, I knew I had achieved my goal of creating "hard fun" (McGonigal, 2011) mentioned in chapter one. For the latest iteration of my coding class, I added a final project presentation where students have to screencast playing the game, explain how they coded the game, and describe what they would do differently if they could go back and do it again, thus making their thinking visible and audible. My hope is that students sharing these final project presentations with other students will provide exemplars for those who have not reached that point, advice for those getting started on their projects, and further a sense of community.

How Can a Boss Level Bring All Skills Together?

The final boss battle should feel like the culmination of all the learning that has taken place in the game—whether that be a commercial videogame or our own curricular games. As Prensky (2011) explains,

> In a high-quality complex game, every skill necessary to be learned and mastered in order to achieve the game's goals is broken down into tiny steps. As players demonstrate repeatedly that they can perform a step, they move up a numerical level in that skill. When certain combinations of individual levels have been reached, players move up to the more "global" levels. Each succeeding level is harder to reach, but it also brings with it better rewards, such as treasure, new abilities, and new places to explore. This makes moving up a desired experience in itself—not to mention that it advances you toward your ultimate goal (which you can only achieve at the highest level).
>
> (p. 274)

As Boller and Kapp (2017) point out, for learning games, "Winning must be contingent upon learning" (p. 26). Asking yourself what evidence you would need to see in order to know that a student achieved the learning objectives will help you think of a final boss battle that will produce that type of evidence. A final project where students are allowed to explore their own interests, express themselves, and be creative while applying the skills learned over the course of the curricular game I find works best. Of course, this should all be in keeping with the game-story. Whether the final project is a debate, putting someone on trial, creating a museum exhibit, presenting evidence that solves a mystery, filming a movie, building something, or any other number of final projects, it should enable students to show off their learning and the rubric should document that learning using rubric labels in keeping with the game.

How Can You Design a Rewarding Win-State?

If designed well, being successful in the final boss battle, creating that final project, or overcoming that final challenge should be its own reward. However, having an additional reward that is in keeping with the game can provide a sense of pleasure and closure. In one of my earlier attempts at this, I created a cutscene that revealed a whole hidden explanation of aliens orchestrating the whole plot to find the best teachers to bring to their planet. That was not a great one, for many reasons, but mainly because it violated the KISS principle—Keep It Simple, Stupid and also because it was completely out of the blue. Another win-state reward revealed that the culprit was twins the whole time, explaining how someone could be in two places at the same time. That one required a whole setup that, again, complicated things. Keep in mind that you aren't writing the next best novel or movie. You don't have to recreate *Planet of the Apes*, where the sand shifts to reveal the Statue of Liberty and rewrites the story in the audience's minds. If you do have something like that up your sleeve that is a natural outcome of your game-story, then go with it! That is awesome! But if it is something that is clearly contrived, avoid it. Instead, think about what would constitute a natural ending to your story. Remember, students are likely to compare your game-story to their other courses, not the latest blockbuster movie or videogame. One type of reward you could embed in your game is something about you (without being unprofessional) that is revealed as part of whatever character you as the teacher play in the story. For example, in my designing curriculum class, the character I play (the vice principal) shows an actual video of me teaching from when I was a high school English teacher and a local news channel filmed me. This final reward also serves as an affirmation that the player, the newbie teacher, is no longer a newbie because they are now a part of the teacher community. Another option for a final reward is a hint at a sequel. You saw how I did this in my coding class, where students see a cutscene that sets up another "save the world by coding" situation that you read about earlier. If you think about these endings in terms of the hero archetype, one possibility is to have the player return to their original world[1] a changed person but you could also have a new call to adventure, such as a trailer that hints at a sequel.

Why Might You Want Your Students to Lose?

Despite all my talk about setting students up for success, sometimes the lesson is in the losing. For example, one of my students designed a game about the Underground Railroad. She wanted to impress upon her students how many people did not make it to show how risky and harrowing it was. I suggested she design a *Choose Your Own Adventure*–type game with many paths that ended badly. Brenda Romero, in her (2012) TED Talk titled "Gaming for Understanding," describes how she created a game to really *teach* her daughter about the Middle Passage after her daughter simply recited facts about the Middle Passage but clearly did not comprehend it. The game that Romero developed involved getting a boat full of people with 30 units of food across a sea in 10 turns, where each turn involved rolling a die and subtracting that amount of food from the total amount. The learning in this game derived from constantly losing the game. Romero enabled her daughter to better understand the Middle Passage by getting her to experience it, well, not "it" but a game designed to demonstrate a key aspect of the Middle Passage. Even if the game itself is not designed to experience an impossible situation by losing, you might have a game where students do end up losing. In that case, Boller and Kapp (2017) recommend "ask[ing] players to find lessons within the loss. Have them analyze why they lost and ask, 'Can those insights lead to learning?'" (p. 27). As Malcolm X observed. "There is no better teacher than adversity. Every defeat, every heartbreak, every loss, contains its own seed, its own lesson on how to improve your performance the next time" (Onion et al., 2009). Remember, the ultimate goal is not winning; it's learning.

What to Do about Early Finishers?

If you have students play your game individually, as partners, or even in small groups, you will be faced with some students who finish before others. One way to utilize those students is to get them to help those who struggle. You can even incorporate them into the story as NPCs, including playing as ghosts. However, there are other approaches as well. You can have side quests, extensions to the game, and various achievements and collectibles for students to try to get. You can even design a game that has different levels of winning. For example, if you create a game about running for an elected office, the goal could be to win; however, one level of winning could be getting a plurality, the next level a majority, and the highest level a mandate. Building a game for replayability is another possibility. For example, the student game I described earlier, where the player chooses different characters from *The Outsiders*, requires students to only play through as one character, but the teacher could offer extra credit to those who do so as more than one character. You can also challenge students to play through to experience all the fail states. In the simulation I created where the player raises a baby, students could find out what happens if you ignore the baby's cries or constantly discourage them from exploring. You can even challenge students to create a game of their own on the topic if they finish early or on a related topic for students in an earlier grade. There are lots of options for early finishers.

How to Debrief in a Way That Cements Lessons Learned?

After the game has concluded, you should have a debriefing session. Part of this should be what is called the After Action Review, described by Michael and Chen (2006) as "review[ing] what was *supposed* to happen, establish[ing] what *actually* happened, determin[ing] what went *right* and *wrong*, and assist[ing] with helping determine how the mission could be *done better* in the future" (p. 66). In other words, players reflect on their own performance, including where they were before they began and where they are now. Interestingly, this sounds a lot like the format of teacher observation reflection meetings. However, you also want students to reflect on the game itself by asking questions like the following:

> How did you make sense of the game within the context of the content area? Are there aspects of this fictional game that are different from reality? What did you learn from playing the game? How could the game be made better? How did learning this material within the context of a game differ, or not, from learning the material in a more traditional way? How does the learning in this game apply to the real world?

Sylvester (2013) suggests "ask[ing] them to tell you the story of what happened" because then you will find out what was important to them (p. 172). You can also ask students about what is not there by asking questions like: "What are other choices the player could have had that are not represented in this game? How would that make gameplay, learning, values, etc. different? What does the game leave unsaid and what does that say?" This is also an opportunity to explore any biases in the game and ethical dilemmas both in and about the game. Making yourself vulnerable by sharing with students what the game design experience was like for you, including some of the decisions you had to make, can help create a space where students feel comfortable being vulnerable and honest with you. This can also give students insight into what you grappled with in terms of designing a curricular game. This debriefing session should allow students to reflect on their own experiences and for you to reflect on how to make the game better for next time, just like how we, as educators, constantly reflect on how to improve our teaching. It also gives you a chance to clear up any misconceptions, make sure students understand how things are in the real world as opposed to the game world, and explain any metaphors or stealth learning you may have used in the game-story. Taking notes or, if you get permission from your students, recording this debriefing session will serve you well. In addition, you should have students fill out their own evaluations in case students get overlooked or do not feel comfortable sharing their true feelings in front of the class.

Conclusion

Just like we end our units with a final test or project that brings everything together, so should your curricular game. However, unlike most curricular units, our curricular game-story needs to end with either some sense of closure or a sense of a possibility for a follow-up curricular game. Keeping in mind the goal of learning can help you design an ending that fits with both the game-story and your learning goals, even if that means having the whole class lose. Debriefing afterward helps students to organize their learning and put it into context. It also gives you a chance to reflect on the game and how you can make changes for next time. More importantly, it can give you a sense of whether or not game-based teaching works for you and your students.

Chapter 7 Worksheet: End States

Directions: Fill out the following chart by describing what the win-state and the lose-state each look like. Add more rows if you have multiple win-states and/or lose-states.

	Description	Lessons Learned	Rewards/ Punishments	Reflection Questions
Win state				
Lose state				

Note

1. In the case of the Designing Curriculum class, this "world" is a bar called the *Thirsty Scholar* that the player went to earlier in the story where the veteran teachers challenged them to a drinking game.

References

Boller, S. & Kapp, K. (2017). *Play to learn: Everything you need to know about designing effective learning games.* Alexandria, VA: ATD Press.

Kellinger, J. (2022). *Coding for non-coders.* In Course taught in the College of Education and Human Development. Boston, MA: UMass Boston.

McGonigal, J. (2011). *Reality is broken: Why games make us better and how they can change the world.* London: Penguin Books.

Michael, D. & Chen, S. (2006). *Serious games: Games that educate, train, and inform.* Boston, MA: Thomson.

Onion, A., Sullivan, M., Mullen, M. & Zapata, C. (2009). Malcolm X. *The History Channel.* Retrieved July 12, 2024 from https://www.history.com/topics/black-history/malcolm-x

Prensky, M. (2011). Comments on research comparing games to other instructional methods. In S. Tobias and J. D. Fletcher (Eds.), *Computer games and instruction* (pp. 251–280). Charlotte, NC: Information Age Publishers.

Romero, B. (2012). Gaming for understanding. *TedTalk*. Retrieved July 12, 2024 from https://www.ted.com/talks/brenda_romero_gaming_for_understanding?subtitle=en&trigger=5s

Sylvester, T. (2013). *Designing games: A guide to engineering experiences*. Sebastopol, CA: O'Reilly Media.

8

Achievement Unlocked!

Sybil:	Look who showed up for the celebration at the Thirsty Scholar! Vice Principal Jackson! Hey, where's your sidekick, Principal Kellinger?
VP Jackson:	You know she doesn't go to these things. She thinks it **blurs the line between boss and employees**.
Jack:	And you?
VP Jackson:	I can think and do what I want (muttering under her breath) most of the time.
VP Jackson (continuing):	Besides, I feel like I'm one of you since I was a teacher at this school once upon a time.
Leonard:	That's right. Remember the time you were on the news?
VP Jackson:	That was one of those days when I didn't feel on my game, but **when the principal asks you to do something…**
Alberta:	Yeah, that was also back in the day when people didn't really follow **FERPA rules** either. I can't believe our previous principal allowed the local news to **show**

	students on TV without getting parental permission! Principal Kellinger would never allow that!
VP Jackson:	Well, I can show it here since it's **not for public consumption**. Do y'all want to reminisce?
Chorus:	*Of course!*
VP Jackson (fumbling with her phone):	*I just can't believe that these students now have jobs and families of their own. Did I tell you I ran into one of my former students at an amusement park? She was there with her kids and she works with my brother-in-law. It was surreal. Ok here's the video. Press the play button below. Enjoy!*

(Kellinger, *Data-Based Planning*, 2010)

The excerpt is the ending of the designing curriculum class that I previously described, where the reward for successfully completing the game is seeing a video of me from when I taught high school. I included this here because it illustrates how stories can teach without being didactic. Notice that it lets students, who are or shortly will be new teachers, know that there is a different relationship between bosses and employees than coworkers have with each other and that employees should do what bosses ask them to do as long as it's ethical. It also reminds students about FERPA (the Family Educational Rights and Privacy Act), something they learned about at the very beginning of the course, by providing an example of a violation and by explaining that making something public has a higher standard.

When students learn about FERPA at the very beginning of this course, they do so by having to pass a professional conduct assessment as part of their teacher interview process without having learned about FERPA. If they answer the FERPA questions wrong, they fail but get an explanation about FERPA and get to try again. If they answer them correctly, they also get a description of FERPA. Cazden (1981) calls this method "performance before competence"—in other words, trying something out before learning about it. At first, that seems antithetical to teaching and a prime way to set students up for failure. However, what it does is it gives students a context and a reason for learning the material. It is the feedback on their performance that develops competence. Some studies show (Shaffer, 2006) that this kind of contextual learning makes long-term retention more likely.

> **ACTION ITEM:** Look through the glossary at the end of this book. All those words are familiar because you encountered them in context while reading this book. If you had been given that list to memorize at the beginning of this book, your chances of understanding those words would be less than they are now. There is one word in the glossary that does not appear in the text of the book. See if you can figure out which one it is.[1]

Gee (2003) demonstrates how powerful "performance before competence" can be by explaining how he tried reading the game manual before playing *Deus Ex* and the manual made no sense. But once he started playing the game, the manual made perfect sense. This was prior to 2003. Notice that videogames nowadays no longer come with game manuals. Videogame companies realized that players prefer to learn the game while playing. In fact, part of the gameplay is learning the rules of the game as feedback from the game tells the players what different actions do. Remember, too, that lack of feedback is also feedback, so if a player clicks on something and nothing happens, then they know that item is not manipulatable. The advantage of learning via gaming versus traditional lectures and disconnected exercises is that games give learning meaning and students motivation as they experience the curriculum instead of just being exposed to it.

How Can You Improve Your Curricular Game?

In the previous chapter, I strongly recommended having a debriefing session after the game concludes. One of the advantages of being a teacher is that we constantly have opportunities to reflect on and improve our teaching every time we teach a class or, sometimes, even on the spot as we change what we did in first period to something we think will work better in our sixth period. For videogame designers, once a game is published, it is published (although now that many games are online, there are periodic updates). Despite our constant refinement, we do want a workable product the first time we teach using a curricular game. For this, we can draw lessons from the videogame industry, which makes extensive use of playtesting. The initial type of testing is called "gray-box" testing. Gray-box testing is when you play your game as a player to see what that experience is like. You probably already do this with some of your curricular materials—for example, taking a test you have designed before you give it to students to make sure the questions are clear and that you don't accidentally make answers too obvious or give away an answer in another question. There are two reasons this is called gray-box testing. One is that a "gray box" is between a black box—when you use a tech tool without understanding the inner workings, for me, this would include my television set—and a white box—when you have designed a tech tool, so you know exactly how it works. In the case of gray-box testing, you, the designer (white box), are experiencing it as if you don't know how the insides work (black box). The second reason it is called gray boxing is because videogame designers sometimes create the initial prototypes of their games using literal gray boxes to represent buildings, items, and even enemies. I am so glad I gray-box tested that "coming to" mini-game I described earlier. I decided to put in a groaning sound to add to the effect of coming to; however, when I gray-box tested it, I realized that the groaning sounded more like noises people make when they are getting intimate. I immediately got rid of the groaning sounds! One of my students in my Introduction to Game-Based Teaching class was shocked by his own inability to notice flaws when he was creating his game after finding several mistakes when he gray-box tested it. You can think of gray-box testing as proofreading. You are looking to make sure everything works like you expect it to, root out little errors, ensure there are no loopholes or places where students will get stuck, and look at the big picture to make sure everything flows, including "asking why" (Nicholson, 2016) about every game element to make sure it is consistent with the game-story and your learning goals. Keep in mind, though, that every single change has a ripple effect. You want to make sure you don't create a new problem when fixing an old one. That is why you need to test and retest.

Gray-box testing is also your opportunity to test your game out in many different venues. You want to design both for usability (a typical student) and for accessibility (a range of students). If it is a digital game, this will mean trying it out on different platforms (Mac and PC), different versions of the software used to run it, and, if it is online, different browsers that students might use. You may even want to see how it renders on phones. Think about common design principles such as making sure you use high contrast, larger and bolder text for more important items, image size and placement, and how "busy" something looks. For accommodations, you want to make sure that there is nothing that requires students to be able to see colors for those who are color blind or visually impaired. Notice I used the word requires. If you use color-coding in your game to distinguish among different levels or categories or types of items, as long as there are other ways to tell them apart, then keep the color-coding as an enhancement. You should, however, always use alternate text on images and videos so students who rely on a screen reader or just have slow computers or internet connection can still know what is on the screen. Again, if it contains something necessary to the game, provide alternate means, such as a transcript, for students to access the content. As teachers, we typically think of accommodations for students who have physical, cognitive, or mental health needs; however, if you are going to expect your students to play your game at home, you should playtest it on devices that are older and slower for students who might not be able to afford the latest and greatest in technology. If you designed an awesome game for students to play as a whole class while in school, you might want to think about ways you could modify it for a student who is out for a long-term illness. You know your student population best. Give some thought to how you can design it for *them*. Even if you don't make all these modifications now because, for example, you know your class does not have any blind students, do give some thought to how you might do that if you need to in the future.

Alpha testing is when you ask a colleague to play your curricular game. Having someone who teaches the same content area you do gives you the opportunity to make sure your content is accurate, to use their teacher lens to assess if it teaches the content, and to make sure the story is coherent. For example, in my coding class, one of the challenges is to mentally code the robot to look out a window to see if it is day or if it is night. My alpha tester pointed out that I did not have an explanation for how the "you" in the story, who, at this point, is bound and gagged on their office floor, could see what the robot saw through the window. The beauty of stories is that you can use them to explain away anything as long as it is consistent and coherent. After my alpha tester pointed that out, I included in the story this line: "Good thing I added that webcam to Sparky that I can mentally see through!" When choosing your alpha tester, make sure they have the expertise you need, that you respect their opinion, that they are someone you are willing to be vulnerable in front of, and that they are someone who is willing to point out your mistakes. In the case of my coding class, my alpha tester is my sister, a software engineer who fits all these requirements.

The last level of testing is beta testing. This is when you test out your game with a sampling of the target audience. As mentioned earlier, as teachers, this happens every time we teach a class. However, before you "go live" with your game, it is helpful to have a small group of students give you feedback. When my children were in elementary school, I had them take a look at a game one of my students had designed in PowerPoint. As they stared and commented on the first slide and then waited and waited, I could not figure out why they were not advancing to the next slide. Finally, one of them asked, "When is this loading screen going to be over?" I had assumed my kids would be able to recognize it as a PowerPoint presentation and know how to advance to the next slide; however, for them, games meant loading screens. One of my students in my Introduction to Game-Based Teaching class thought that giving her students free rein would be skill-based but discovered that free rein was too much for them, and students ended up randomly clicking, making gameplay simple chance. Beta testing helps reveal your own assumptions and makes it clear where you need to provide more guidance, give more clarity, adjust the amount of information, and make any number of other changes to increase the learning and enhance the fun.

When you beta test, there are some steps you might want to take. For example, you might want to give your beta testers a pretest and a posttest on the topic to measure if and what they actually learned. While they are playtesting, if possible, you should observe them. If they are randomly pointing and clicking, then you know you have not made the decisions "partially predictable" (Sylvester, 2013, p. 123), and you need to provide more information. If they are quickly clicking through the game and getting to the end, you know you have either provided too much information or created a game where players can choose any response and get to the end. The second can be acceptable if it is a game of judgment calls; however, if players are just clicking through, that means you have not devised ways for them to reflect on their decisions. Requiring students to keep a field journal or some other means of recording their thoughts as a part of the gameplay can be invaluable in this regard as long as it does not appear contrived; otherwise, it will be seen as getting in the way of gameplaying. You can also do some out-of-game reflection, such as reserving the last five minutes of class for students to fill out exit tickets, which might be as simple as asking what students plan to do next and why so you can capture their thinking or assign homework where they reflect on their gameplay. You can also slow down gameplay to make students give more thought than trial and error to their game decisions by putting students in small groups and requiring consensus or unanimity. You can also put students in driver/navigator partnerships where the navigator tells the driver what to do with allowance for discussion. If you do this, make sure they switch roles every lesson. When you observe your playtesters play, be sure to also notice where they look and what they click on. Observation can tell you a lot about how a player approaches a game:

> Nothing is quite as humbling as being forced to watch in silence as some poor play-tester stumbles around your level for 20 minutes unable to figure out the "obvious" answer that you now realize is completely arbitrary and impossible to figure out.
>
> (Birdwell, 1999/2006, p 219)

Playtesting means making yourself vulnerable. However, as a teacher, you already know what that feels like!

You don't want to slow down gameplay by peppering your playtesters with questions while they play because that is artificial and distracting, but you can ask them to think out loud while they play. This is common among videogame players and a feature of popular videos of people playing videogames, so this will be considered acceptable. When playtesters are done playing, asking what they think the learning objectives are and what they actually learned can tell you a lot about whether or not your curricular game achieved your goals. You can also take the plus/delta approach by asking your testers what they liked and why and what they would change and why. If you have the chance to observe them play, you can consult your notes to ask them about their strategies or why they made particular moves. If there are any places where they appeared to be stuck or confused, ask them what they were thinking, how they got unstuck, and if there is anything that would have helped them get unstuck sooner. Asking playtesters about the moral and ethical dimensions of the game can be revealing as well. For example, finding out what messages they took from the game and how those lessons would impact their future behavior can be helpful. Asking them what they think they will remember about the experience five or ten years from now can help you tap into the "enduring understandings" (Wiggins and McTighe, 1998) they took from the game. Finally, although this can be scary, asking if they found the experience fun and what you could do to make it more fun will allow you to get some ideas from your students. What can be as important as feedback is students feeling like their input matters. However, obviously, you do have the final say. If students suggest something beyond your technological abilities or that you deem unnecessary, distracting, or the opposite of your learning goals, you need to use your own discretion.

How Can You Know If Your Curricular Game Was Effective?

Through the playtesting process—both before you launch the game and the ongoing playtesting that having new students every year affords—you will be able to gather a lot of data about your curricular game. You know your curricular goals and are in the best position to assess whether or not they have been met—for example, if students start talking about history in terms of patterns of cause and effect instead of as discrete historical events. However, there are other indicators as well. For example, if students are talking about your game outside of your classroom, like the teacher Klopfer (2008) describes as overhearing her typically most disengaged students excitedly discussing who got "sick" and how in the hallways when playing the Virus game, you will know you have been successful. One of my own students said that when they played the game they designed in my class with their students, engagement went from "zero to fun." Observation is often the best assessment of success.

How Can You Spread the Word?

You may be familiar with the SAMR model of technological adoption—Substitution, Augmentation, Modification, and Redefinition. Game-based teaching, whether you use technology or not, goes beyond the SAMR model to completely transform your teaching and student learning. If you are successful at finding the fun in learning through game-based teaching, word will get around. I have had several students tell me they are taking my class because a friend recommended it. If you are a beginner at game design, you may want to find someone who is like-minded to take this plunge with you. If you have designed curricular games for a while, you might want to take someone under your wing and guide them while they develop their first curricular game. One of my former students, Sandra Schwarzkopf who designed the *Foresight* game you were introduced to in Chapter 4, was so inspired by game-based teaching that she and her colleague started a nonprofit to help others design game-based curriculum called Gamepossible Learning at https://gamepossible.org. Wherever you are in your journey, bringing others along can transform not only your teaching but also transform teaching overall. And you might learn something new from others!

Conclusion

I view teaching and learning as a journey, trying different paths and learning along the way. I hope you have enjoyed taking this journey with me and that you bring others along. Just like in good videogames, trying something out, getting feedback, and making changes accordingly will help you calibrate your game-based teaching to who you are as a teacher and your own students' needs and wants. You will make mistakes along the way, just as I have laid bare several mistakes I have made. But remember, just like gameplaying is about learning from mistakes, so is game-based teaching. In the words of my father, I wish you good skill.

Chapter 8 Worksheet: Playtesting

Directions: For each type of testing, record your observations and feedback from your testers. Based on this feedback, think about what changes you should make to your game. Be sure to test again after making those changes.

	Observations and Feedback	Changes to Game
Gray-box testing		
Alpha testing		
Beta testing		

Note

1. The word is "rubberbanding."

References

Birdwell, K. (1999/2006). The Cabal: Valve's design process for creating Half-Life. In K. Salen & E. Zimmerman (Eds.), *The game designer reader: A rules of play anthology* (pp. 212–225) Cambridge, MA: MIT Press.

Cazden, C. (1981). Performance before competence: Assistance to child discourse in the zone of proximal development. *Quarterly Newsletter of the Laboratory of Comparative Human Cognition, 3*, 5–8.

Gee, J. P. (2003). *What videogames have to teach us about learning and literacy*. New York: Palgrave Macmillan.

Kellinger, J. (2010). *Data-based planning*. UMass Boston.

Klopfer, E. (2008). *Augmented learning: Research and design of mobile educational games*. Cambridge, MA: MIT Press.

Nicholson, Scott. (2016). Ask why: Creating a better player experience through environmental storytelling and consistency in escape room design. Paper Presented at *Meaningful Play 2016*, Lansing, Michigan. Available at http://scottnicholson.com/pubs/askwhy.pdf [Retrieved July 21, 2024].

Shaffer, D. W. (2006). *How computer games help children learn*. New York: Palgrave MacMillan.

Sylvester, T. (2013). *Designing games: A guide to engineering experiences*. Sebastopol, CA: O'Reilly Media.

Wiggins, G. & McTighe, J. (1998). *Understanding by design*. Alexandria, VA: ASCD.

Glossary

achievers—a type of videogame player characterized by gaining pleasure from success

alpha testing—asking peers to give you feedback on your game

agent—a character controlled by computer programming

avatar—a character controlled by a human being

beta testing—using the target demographic, in our case our students, to test a game

boss fight—a challenge where a player tries to defeat an enemy

COTS—commercial-off-the-shelf, i.e. products (in this case games) that you can buy

curricular game—a game whose goal is to teach a specific curricular unit or lesson

Easter eggs—hidden items in a game where users need to click on a specific area to reveal them

explorers—a type of videogame player who likes to explore their environment and test its limitations

golden path—the optimal path through a game story to get to a win-state

gray-box testing—a game designer playing their own game in order to "proofread" it

killers—a type of videogame player who likes to dominate

levels—the various stages of a game that get increasingly more difficult

NPCs—non-playable characters—these are all the other characters in a game besides the one the player is playing

playtesting—having people play early stages of your game in order to get feedback and make changes *promotyping*—testing an idea by running it by students to see what they think

rubberbanding—a game mechanism that gives players who are behind a chance to catch up

socializers—a type of player who likes to interact with others

For Product Safety Concerns and Information please contact our EU representative GPSR@taylorandfrancis.com
Taylor & Francis Verlag GmbH, Kaufingerstraße 24, 80331 München, Germany

www.ingramcontent.com/pod-product-compliance
Lightning Source LLC
Chambersburg PA
CBHW052341230426
43664CB00041B/2600